Chernobyl disaster

This is about the 1986 nuclear plant accident in Ukraine.

Chernobyl disaster

The nuclear reactor after the disaster. Reactor 4 (center). Turbine building (lower left). Reactor 3 (center right).

Date	26 April 1986
Time	01:23 (Moscow Time UTC+3)
Location	Pripyat, (former Ukrainian SSR, Soviet Union)

1

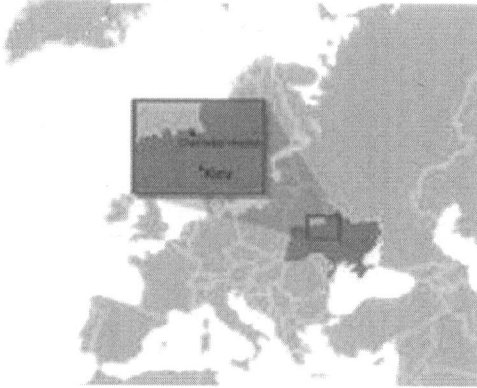

Location of Chernobyl nuclear power plant

The abandoned city of <u>Pripyat</u> with Chernobyl plant in the distance

The **Chernobyl disaster** (<u>Ukrainian</u>: Чорнобильська катастрофа, *Chornobylska Katastrofa – Chornobyl Catastrophe*) was a <u>catastrophic</u> <u>nuclear accident</u> that occurred on 26 April 1986 at the <u>Chernobyl Nuclear Power Plant</u> in Ukraine (then officially the <u>Ukrainian SSR</u>), which was under the direct jurisdiction of the central authorities of the <u>Soviet Union</u>. An explosion and fire released large quantities of radioactive particles into the atmosphere, which spread over much of the western USSR and <u>Europe</u>.

The Chernobyl disaster is widely considered to have been the worst nuclear power plant accident in history, and is one of only two classified as a level 7 event (the maximum classification) on the International Nuclear Event Scale (the other being the Fukushima Daiichi nuclear disaster in 2011).[1] The battle to contain the contamination and avert a greater catastrophe ultimately involved over 500,000 workers and cost an estimated 18 billion rubles.[2] The official Soviet casualty count of 31 deaths has been disputed, and long-term effects such as cancers and deformities are still being accounted for.

Table of Contents

Overview

The disaster began during a systems test on Saturday, 26 April 1986 at reactor number four of the Chernobyl plant, which is near the city of Pripyat and in proximity to the administrative border with Belarus and the Dnieper river. There was a sudden and unexpected power surge, and when an emergency shutdown was attempted, an exponentially larger spike in power output occurred, which led to a reactor vessel rupture and a series of steam explosions. These events exposed the graphite moderator of the reactor to air, causing it to ignite.[3] The resulting fire sent a plume of highly radioactive fallout into the atmosphere and over an extensive geographical area, including Pripyat. The plume drifted over large parts of the western Soviet Union and Europe. From 1986 to 2000, 350,400 people were evacuated and resettled from the most severely contaminated areas of Belarus, Russia, and Ukraine.[4][5] According to official post-Soviet data,[6][7] about 60% of the fallout landed in Belarus.

The accident raised concerns about the safety of the Soviet nuclear power industry, as well as nuclear power in general, slowing its expansion for a number of years and forcing the Soviet government to become less secretive about its procedures.[8][notes 1] The government cover-up of the Chernobyl disaster was a "catalyst" for glasnost, which "paved the way for reforms leading to the Soviet collapse".[9]

Russia, Ukraine, and Belarus have been burdened with the continuing and substantial decontamination and health care costs of the Chernobyl accident. A report by the International Atomic Energy Agency examines the environmental consequences of the accident.[7] Another UN agency, UNSCEAR, has estimated a global collective dose of radiation exposure from the accident "equivalent on average to 21 additional days of world exposure to natural background radiation"; individual doses were far higher than the global mean among those most exposed, including 530,000 local recovery workers who averaged an effective dose equivalent to an extra 50 years of typical natural background radiation exposure each.[10][11][12] Estimates of the number of deaths that will eventually result from the accident vary enormously; disparities reflect both the lack of solid scientific data and the different methodologies used to quantify mortality – whether the discussion is confined to specific geographical areas or extends worldwide, and whether the deaths are immediate, short term, or long term.

Thirty one deaths are directly attributed to the accident, all among the reactor staff and emergency workers.[13] An UNSCEAR report places the total confirmed deaths from radiation at 64 as of 2008. The Chernobyl Forum predicts the eventual death toll could reach 4,000 among those exposed to the highest levels of radiation (200,000 emergency workers, 116,000 evacuees and 270,000 residents of the most contaminated areas); this figure is a total causal death toll prediction, combining the deaths of approximately 50 emergency workers who died soon after the accident from acute radiation syndrome, nine children who have died of thyroid cancer and a future predicted total of 3940 deaths from radiation-induced cancer and leukemia.[14]

In a peer reviewed publication in the International Journal of Cancer in 2006, the authors of which, following a different conclusion methodology to the Chernobyl forum study, which arrived at the total predicted, 4000, death toll after cancer survival rates were factored in, the paper stated, without entering into a discussion on deaths, that in terms of total excess cancers attributed to the accident:[15]

The risk projections suggest that by now Chernobyl may have caused about 1,000 cases of thyroid cancer and 4,000 cases of other cancers in Europe, representing about 0.01% of all incident cancers since the accident. Models predict that by 2065 about 16,000 cases of thyroid cancer and 25,000 cases of other cancers may be expected due to radiation from the accident, whereas several hundred million cancer cases are expected from other causes.

Also based upon extrapolations from the linear no-threshold model of radiation induced damage, down to zero, the Union of Concerned Scientists estimates that, among the hundreds of millions of people living in broader geographical areas, there will be 50,000 excess cancer cases resulting in 25,000 excess cancer deaths.[16]

For this broader group, the 2006 TORCH report, commissioned by the European Greens political party, predicts 30,000 to 60,000 excess cancer deaths.[17] In terms of non-scientific publications, two affiliated with the anti-nuclear advocacy group Greenpeace, have been released, one of which reports the figure at 200,000 or more.[18]

The Russian founder of that region's chapter of Greenpeace also authored a book titled *Chernobyl: Consequences of the Catastrophe for People and the Environment*, which concludes that among the billions of people worldwide who were exposed to radioactive contamination from the disaster, nearly a million premature cancer deaths occurred between 1986 and 2004.[19] The book, however, has failed the peer review process.[20][21] Of the five reviews published in the academic press, four considered the book severely flawed and contradictory, and one praised it while noting some shortcomings. The review by M. I. Balonov published by the New York Academy of Sciences concludes that the report is of negative value because it has very little scientific merit while being highly misleading to the lay reader. It characterized the estimate of nearly a million deaths as more in the realm of science fiction than science.[22]

Accident

On 26 April 1986, at 01:23 (UTC+3), reactor four suffered a catastrophic power increase, leading to explosions in its core. This dispersed large quantities of radioactive fuel and core materials into the atmosphere [23]:73 and ignited the combustible graphite moderator. The burning graphite moderator increased the emission of radioactive particles, carried by the smoke, as the reactor had not been encased by any kind of hard containment vessel. The accident occurred during an experiment scheduled to test a potential safety emergency core cooling feature, which took place during a normal shutdown procedure.

Steam turbine tests

An inactive nuclear reactor continues to generate a significant amount of residual decay heat. In an initial shutdown state (for example, following an emergency SCRAM) the reactor produces around 7 percent of its total thermal output and requires cooling to avoid core damage. RBMK reactors, like those at Chernobyl, use water as a coolant.[24][25] Reactor 4 at Chernobyl consisted of about 1,600 individual fuel channels; each required a coolant flow of 28 metric tons (28,000 liters or 7,400 U.S. gallons) per hour.[23]

Since cooling pumps require electricity to cool a reactor after a SCRAM, in the event of a power grid failure, Chernobyl's reactors had three backup diesel generators; these could start up in 15 seconds, but took 60–75 seconds[23]:15 to attain full speed and reach the 5.5-megawatt (MW) output required to run one main pump.[23]:30

To solve this one-minute gap, considered an unacceptable safety risk, it had been theorized that rotational energy from the steam turbine (as it wound down under residual steam pressure) could be used to generate the required electrical power. Analysis indicated that this residual momentum and steam pressure might be sufficient to run the coolant pumps for 45 seconds,[23]:16 bridging the gap between an external power failure and the full availability of the emergency generators.[26]

This capability still needed to be confirmed experimentally, and previous tests had ended unsuccessfully. An initial test carried out in 1982 showed that the excitation voltage of the turbine-generator was insufficient; it did not maintain the desired magnetic field after the turbine trip. The system was modified, and the test was repeated in 1984 but again proved unsuccessful. In 1985, the tests were attempted a third time but also yielded negative results. The test procedure was to be repeated again in 1986, and it was scheduled to take place during the maintenance shutdown of Reactor Four.[26]

The test focused on the switching sequences of the electrical supplies for the reactor. The test procedure was to begin with an automatic emergency shutdown. No detrimental effect on the safety of the reactor was anticipated, so the test program was not formally coordinated with either the chief designer of the reactor (NIKIET) or the scientific manager. Instead, it was approved only by the director of the plant (and even this approval was not consistent with established procedures).[27]

According to the test parameters, the thermal output of the reactor should have been *no lower* than 700 MW at the start of the experiment. If test conditions had been as planned, the procedure would almost certainly have been carried out safely; the eventual disaster resulted from attempts to boost the reactor output once the experiment had been started, which was inconsistent with approved procedure.[27]

The Chernobyl power plant had been in operation for two years without the capability to ride through the first 60–75 seconds of a total loss of electric power, and thus lacked an important safety feature. The station managers presumably wished to correct this at the first opportunity, which may explain why they continued the test even when serious problems arose, and why the requisite approval for the test had not been sought from the Soviet nuclear oversight regulator (even though there was a representative at the complex of 4 reactors).[notes 2]:18–20

The experimental procedure was intended to run as follows:

1. The reactor was to be running at a low power level, between 700 MW and 800 MW.
2. The steam-turbine generator was to be run up to full speed.
3. When these conditions were achieved, the steam supply for the turbine generator was to be closed off.
4. Turbine generator performance was to be recorded to determine whether it could provide the bridging power for coolant pumps until the emergency diesel generators were sequenced to start and provide power to the cooling pumps automatically.
5. After the emergency generators reached normal operating speed and voltage, the turbine generator would be allowed to freewheel down.

Conditions before the accident

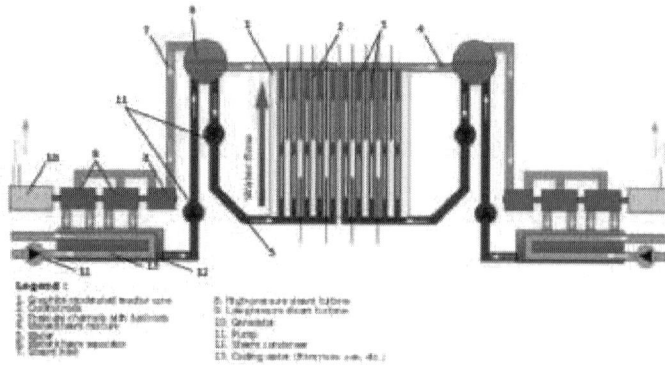

A schematic diagram of the reactor

The conditions to run the test were established before the day shift of 25 April 1986. The day shift workers had been instructed in advance and were familiar with the established procedures. A special team of electrical engineers was present to test the new voltage regulating system.[28] As planned, a gradual reduction in the output of the power unit was begun at 01:06 on 25 April, and the power level had reached 50% of its nominal 3200 MW thermal level by the beginning of the day shift.

At this point, another regional power station unexpectedly went offline, and the Kiev electrical grid controller requested that the further reduction of Chernobyl's output be postponed, as power was needed to satisfy the peak evening demand. The Chernobyl plant director agreed, and postponed the test. Despite this postponement, preparations for the test not affecting the reactor's power were carried out, including the disabling of the emergency core cooling system or ECCS, a passive/active system of core cooling intended to provide water to the core in a loss-of-coolant accident. Given the other events that unfolded, the system would have been of limited use, but its disabling as a "routine" step of the test is an illustration of the inherent lack of attention to safety for this test.[29] In addition, had the reactor been shut down for the day as planned, it is possible that more preparation would have been taken in advance of the test.

At 23:04, the Kiev grid controller allowed the reactor shut-down to resume. This delay had some serious consequences: the day shift had long since departed, the evening shift was also preparing to leave, and the night shift would not take over until midnight, well into the job. According to plan, the test should have been finished during the day shift, and the night shift would only have had to maintain decay heat cooling systems in an otherwise shut down plant.[23]:36–8

The night shift had very limited time to prepare for and carry out the experiment. A further rapid reduction in the power level from 50% was executed during the shift change-over. Alexander Akimov was chief of the night shift, and Leonid Toptunov was the operator responsible for the reactor's operational regimen, including the movement of the control rods. Toptunov was a young engineer who had worked independently as a senior engineer for approximately three months.[23]:36–8

The test plan called for a gradual reduction in power output from reactor 4 to a thermal level of 700–1000 MW.[30] An output of 700 MW was reached at 00:05 on 26 April. However, due to the natural production of xenon-135, a neutron absorber, core power continued to decrease without further operator action—a process known as reactor poisoning. As the reactor power output dropped further, to approximately 500 MW, Toptunov mistakenly inserted the

13

control rods too far—the exact circumstances leading to this are unknown because Akimov and Toptunov died in the hospital on May 10 and 14, respectively. This combination of factors rendered the reactor in an unintended near-shutdown state, with a power output of 30 MW thermal or less.

The reactor was now only producing around 5 percent of the minimum initial power level established as safe for the test.[27]:73 Control-room personnel consequently made the decision to restore power by disabling the automatic system governing the control rods and manually extracting the majority of the reactor control rods to their upper limits.[31] Several minutes elapsed between their extraction and the point that the power output began to increase and subsequently stabilize at 160–200 MW (thermal), a much smaller value than the planned 700 MW. The rapid reduction in the power during the initial shutdown, and the subsequent operation at a level of less than 200 MW led to increased poisoning of the reactor core by the accumulation of xenon-135.[32][33] This restricted any further rise of reactor power, and made it necessary to extract additional control rods from the reactor core in order to counteract the poisoning.

The operation of the reactor at the low power level and high poisoning level was accompanied by unstable core temperature and coolant flow, and possibly by instability of neutron flux. Various alarms started going off at this point. The control room received repeated emergency signals regarding the levels in the steam/water separator drums, and large excursions or variations in the flow rate of feed water, as well as from relief valves opened to relieve excess steam into a turbine condenser, and from the neutron power controller. In the period between 00:35 and 00:45, emergency alarm signals concerning thermal-hydraulic parameters were ignored, apparently to preserve the reactor power level.[34]

After a while, a more or less stable state at a power level of 200 MW was achieved, and preparation for the experiment continued. As part of the test plan, extra water pumps were activated at 01:05 on 26 April, increasing the water flow. The increased coolant flow rate through the reactor produced an increase in the inlet coolant temperature of the reactor core (the coolant no longer having sufficient time to release its heat in the turbine and cooling towers), which now more closely approached the nucleate boiling temperature of water, reducing the safety margin.

The flow exceeded the allowed limit at 01:19, triggering an alarm of low steam pressure in the steam separators. At the same time, the extra water flow lowered the overall core temperature and reduced the existing steam voids in the core and the steam separators.[35] Since water also absorbs neutrons (and the higher density of liquid water makes it a better absorber than steam), turning on additional pumps decreased the reactor power further still. The crew responded by turning off two of the circulation pumps to reduce feedwater flow, in an effort to increase steam pressure, and also to remove more manual control rods to maintain power.[29][36]

All these actions led to an extremely unstable reactor configuration. Nearly all of the control rods were removed manually, including all but 9 of the "fail-safe" manually operated rods, which were intended to remain fully inserted to control the reaction even in the event of a loss of coolant. While the emergency SCRAM system that would insert all control rods to shut down the reactor could still be activated manually, the automated system that could do the same had been disabled to maintain power, and many other

15

automated and even passive safety features of the reactor had been bypassed. Further, the reactor coolant had reduced boiling, reducing steam voids, but had limited margin to boiling, so any power excursion would produce boiling, reducing neutron absorption by the water. The reactor was in an unstable configuration that was clearly outside the safe operating envelope established by the designers.

Experiment and explosion

Aerial view of the damaged core on 3 May 1986. Roof of the turbine hall is damaged (image center). Roof of the adjacent reactor 3 (image lower left) shows minor fire damage.

At 1:23:04 a.m. the experiment began. Four of the Main Circulating Pumps (MCP) were active; of the eight total, six are normally active during regular operation. The steam to the turbines was shut off, beginning a run-down of the turbine generator. The diesel generator started and sequentially picked up loads; the generators were to have completely picked up the MCPs' power needs by 01:23:43. In the interim, the power for the MCPs was to be supplied by the turbine generator as it coasted down. As the momentum of the turbine generator decreased, however, so did the power it produced for the pumps. The water flow rate decreased, leading to increased formation of steam voids (bubbles) in the core.

Because of the positive void coefficient of the RBMK reactor at low reactor power levels, it was now primed to embark on a positive feedback loop, in which the formation of steam voids reduced the ability of the liquid water coolant to absorb neutrons, which in turn increased the reactor's power output. This caused yet more water to flash into steam, giving yet a further power increase. During almost the entire period of the experiment the automatic control system successfully counteracted this positive feedback, continuously inserting control rods into the reactor core to limit the power rise. However, this system had control of only 12 rods, and nearly all others had been manually retracted.

At 1:23:40, as recorded by the SKALA centralized control system, an emergency shutdown of the reactor, which inadvertently triggered the explosion, was initiated. The SCRAM was started when the EPS-5 button (also known as the AZ-5 button) of the reactor emergency protection system was pressed: this engaged the drive mechanism on all control rods to fully insert them, including the manual control rods that had been incautiously withdrawn earlier. The reason why the EPS-5 button was pressed is not known, whether it was done as an emergency measure in response to rising temperatures, or simply as a routine method of shutting down the reactor upon completion of the experiment.

There is a view that the SCRAM may have been ordered as a response to the unexpected rapid power increase, although there is no recorded data conclusively proving this. Some have suggested that the button was not pressed, and instead the signal was automatically produced by the emergency protection system; however, the SKALA clearly registered a manual SCRAM signal. In spite of this, the question as to when or even whether the EPS-5 button was pressed has been the subject of debate. There are assertions that the pressure was caused by the rapid power acceleration at the start, and allegations that the button was not pressed until the reactor began to self-destruct but others assert that it happened earlier and in calm conditions.[37]:578[38]

After the EPS-5 button was pressed, the insertion of control rods into the reactor core began. The control rod insertion mechanism moved the rods at 0.4 m/s, so that the rods took 18 to 20 seconds to travel the full height of the core, about 7 meters. A bigger problem was a flawed graphite-tip control rod design, which initially displaced neutron-absorbing coolant with moderating graphite before introducing replacement neutron-absorbing boron material to slow the reaction. As a result, the SCRAM actually increased the reaction rate in the upper half of the core as the tips displaced water. This behavior was known after a shutdown of another RBMK reactor induced an initial power spike, but as the SCRAM of that reactor was successful, the information was not widely disseminated.

A few seconds after the start of the SCRAM, the graphite rod tips entered the fuel pile. A massive power spike occurred, and the core overheated, causing some of the fuel rods to fracture, blocking the control rod columns and jamming the control rods at one-third insertion, with the graphite tips in the middle of the core. Within three seconds the reactor output rose above 530 MW.[23]:31

The subsequent course of events was not registered by instruments; it is known only as a result of mathematical simulation. Apparently, the power spike caused an increase in fuel temperature and massive steam buildup, leading to a rapid increase in steam pressure. This caused the fuel cladding to fail, releasing the fuel elements into the coolant, and rupturing the channels in which these elements were located.[39]

Then, according to some estimations, the reactor jumped to around 30,000 MW thermal, ten times the normal operational output. The last reading on the control panel was 33,000 MW. It was not possible to reconstruct the precise sequence of the processes that led to the destruction of the reactor and the power unit building, but a steam explosion, like the explosion of a steam boiler from excess vapor pressure, appears to have been the next event. There is a general understanding that it was steam from the wrecked fuel channels escaping into the reactor's exterior cooling structure that caused the destruction of the reactor casing, tearing off and lifting the 2,000-ton upper plate, to which the entire reactor assembly is fastened, sending it through the roof of the reactor building. Apparently, this was the first explosion that many heard.[40]:366 This explosion ruptured further fuel channels, as well as severing most of the coolant lines feeding the reactor chamber, and as a result the remaining coolant flashed to steam and escaped the reactor core. The total water loss in combination with a high positive void coefficient further increased the reactor's thermal power.

A second, more powerful explosion occurred about two or three seconds after the first; this explosion dispersed the damaged core and effectively terminated the nuclear chain reaction. However, this explosion also compromised more of the reactor containment vessel and ejected superheated lumps of graphite moderator. The ejected graphite and the demolished channels still in the remains of the reactor vessel caught fire on exposure to air, greatly contributing to the spread of radioactive fallout and the contamination of outlying areas.[41]

According to observers outside Unit 4, burning lumps of material and sparks shot into the air above the reactor. Some of them fell onto the roof of the machine hall and started a fire. About 25 percent of the red-hot graphite blocks and overheated material from the fuel channels was ejected. Parts of the graphite blocks and fuel channels were out of the reactor building. As a result of the damage to the building an airflow through the core was established by the high temperature of the core. The air ignited the hot graphite and started a graphite fire.[23]:32

There were initially several hypotheses about the nature of the second explosion. One view was that the second explosion was caused by hydrogen, which had been produced either by the overheated steam-zirconium reaction or by the reaction of red-hot graphite with steam that produced hydrogen and carbon monoxide. Another hypothesis was that the second explosion was a thermal explosion of the reactor as a result of the uncontrollable escape of fast neutrons caused by the complete water loss in the reactor core.[42] A third hypothesis was that the explosion was a second steam explosion. According to this version, the first explosion was a more minor steam explosion in the circulating loop, causing a loss of coolant flow and pressure that in turn caused the water still in the core to flash to steam. This second explosion then did the majority of the damage to the reactor and containment building.

However, the sheer force of the second explosion, and the ratio of xenon radioisotopes released during the event, indicate that the second explosion could have been a nuclear power transient; the result of the melting core material, in the absence of its cladding, water coolant and moderator, undergoing runaway prompt criticality similar to the explosion of a fizzled nuclear weapon.[43] This nuclear excursion released 40 billion joules of energy, the equivalent of about ten tons of TNT. The analysis indicates that the nuclear excursion was limited to a small portion of the core.[43]

Contrary to safety regulations, bitumen, a combustible material, had been used in the construction of the roof of the reactor building and the turbine hall. Ejected material ignited at least five fires on the roof of the adjacent reactor 3, which was still operating. It was imperative to put those fires out and protect the cooling systems of reactor 3.[23]:42 Inside reactor 3, the chief of the night shift, Yuri Bagdasarov, wanted to shut down the reactor immediately, but chief engineer Nikolai Fomin would not allow this. The operators were given respirators and potassium iodide tablets and told to continue working. At 05:00, however, Bagdasarov made his own decision to shut down the reactor, leaving only those operators there who had to work the emergency cooling systems.[23]:44

Radiation levels

Approximate radiation levels at different locations shortly after the explosion were as follows:[44]

Location	Radiation (Roentgens per hour)	Sieverts per hour (SI Unit)
Vicinity of the reactor core	30,000	300
Fuel fragments	15,000–20,000	150–200
Debris heap at the place of circulation pumps	10,000	100
Debris near the electrolyzers	5,000–15,000	50–150
Water in the Level +25 feedwater room	5,000	50
Level 0 of the turbine hall	500–15,000	5–150
Area of the affected unit	1,000–1,500	10–15
Water in Room 712	1,000	10
Control room	3–5	0.03–0.05
Gidroelektromontazh depot	30	0.3
Nearby concrete mixing unit	10–15	0.10–0.15

Plant layout

Based on the image of the plant[45]

Level	Objects
Metres	Levels are distances above (or below for minus values) ground level at the site.

49.6	Roof of the reactor building, gallery of the refueling mechanism
39.9	Roof of the deaerator gallery
35.5	Floor of the main reactor hall
31.6	Upper side of the upper biological shield, floor of the space for pipes to steam separators
28.3	Lower side of the turbine hall roof
24.0	Deaerator floor, measurement and control instruments room
16.4	Floor of the pipe aisle in the deaerator gallery
12.0	Main floor of the turbine hall, floor of the main circulation pump motor compartments
10.0	Control room, floor under the reactor lower biological shield, main circulation pumps
6.0	Steam distribution corridor
2.2	Upper pressure suppression pool
0.0	Ground level; house switchgear, turbine hall level
−0.5	Lower pressure suppression pool
−5.2, −4.2	Other turbine hall levels
−6.5	Basement floor of the turbine hall

Immediate crisis management

Radiation levels

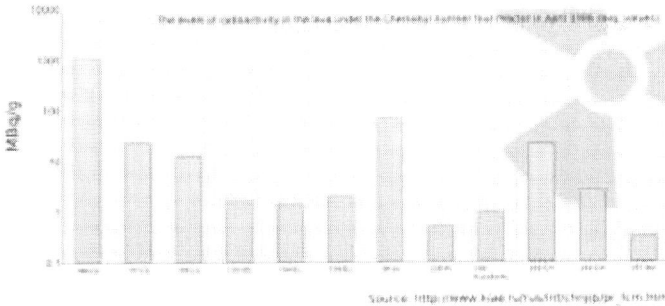

Source: http://www.hse.nwl.ac.uk/rbs.hippta/pe_4r.rn.html

Extremely high levels of radioactivity in the lava under the Chernobyl number four reactor in 1986

The radiation levels in the worst-hit areas of the reactor building have been estimated to be 5.6 roentgens per second (R/s) (1.4 milliamperes per kilogram), equivalent to more than 20,000 roentgens per hour. A lethal dose is around 500 roentgens (5Gy, 0.13 coulombs per kilogram) over 5 hours, so in some areas, unprotected workers received fatal doses in less than a minute. However, a dosimeter capable of measuring up to 1,000 R/s (0.3 A/kg) was buried in the rubble of a collapsed part of the building, and another one failed when turned on. All remaining dosimeters had limits of 0.001 R/s (0.3 µA/kg) and therefore read "off scale". Thus, the reactor crew could ascertain only that the radiation levels were somewhere above 0.001 R/s (3.6 R/h, or 0.3 µA/kg), while the true levels were much higher in some areas.[23]:42–50

Because of the inaccurate low readings, the reactor crew chief Alexander Akimov assumed that the reactor was intact. The evidence of pieces of graphite and reactor fuel

25

lying around the building was ignored, and the readings of another dosimeter brought in by 04:30 were dismissed under the assumption that the new dosimeter must have been defective.[23]:42–50 Akimov stayed with his crew in the reactor building until morning, sending members of his crew to try to pump water into the reactor. None of them wore any protective gear. Most, including Akimov, died from radiation exposure within three weeks.[46]:247–48

Fire containment

Firefighter <u>Leonid Telyatnikov</u>, being decorated for bravery

Shortly after the accident, firefighters arrived to try to extinguish the fires. First on the scene was a Chernobyl Power Station firefighter brigade under the command of Lieutenant Volodymyr Pravik, who died on 9 May 1986 of <u>acute radiation sickness</u>. They were not told how dangerously radioactive the smoke and the debris were, and may not even have known that the accident was anything more than a regular <u>electrical fire</u>: "We didn't know it was the reactor. No one had told us."[47]

Grigorii Khmel, the driver of one of the <u>fire engines</u>, later described what happened:

We arrived there at 10 or 15 minutes to two in the morning.... We saw graphite scattered about. Misha asked: "Is that graphite?" I kicked it away. But one of the fighters on the other truck picked it up. "It's hot," he said. The pieces of graphite were of different sizes, some big, some small, enough to pick them up...

We didn't know much about radiation. Even those who worked there had no idea. There was no water left in the trucks. Misha filled a cistern and we aimed the water at the top. Then those boys who died went up to the roof – Vashchik, Kolya and others, and Volodya Pravik.... They went up the ladder ... and I never saw them again.[48]:54

However, Anatoli Zakharov, a fireman stationed in Chernobyl since 1980, offers a different description:

I remember joking to the others, "There must be an incredible amount of radiation here. We'll be lucky if we're all still alive in the morning."

Twenty years after the disaster, he said the firefighters from the Fire Station No. 2 were aware of the risks.

Of course we knew! If we'd followed regulations, we would never have gone near the reactor. But it was a moral obligation – our duty. We were like kamikaze.[49]

The immediate priority was to extinguish fires on the roof of the station and the area around the building containing Reactor No. 4 to protect No. 3 and keep its core cooling systems intact. The fires were extinguished by 5:00, but many firefighters received high doses of radiation. The fire inside reactor 4 continued to burn until 10 May 1986; it is possible that well over half of the graphite burned out.[23]:73

The fire was extinguished by a combined effort of helicopters dropping over 5,000 metric tons of sand, lead, clay, and neutron-absorbing boron onto the burning reactor and injection of liquid nitrogen. The Ukrainian filmmaker Vladimir Shevchenko captured film footage of an Mi-8 helicopter as its main rotor collided with a nearby construction crane cable, causing the helicopter to fall near the damaged reactor building and killing its four-man crew.[50] It is now known that virtually none of the neutron absorbers reached the core.[51]

From eyewitness accounts of the firefighters involved before they died (as reported on the CBC television series *Witness*), one described his experience of the radiation as "tasting like metal", and feeling a sensation similar to that of pins and needles all over his face. (This is similar to the description given by Louis Slotin, a Manhattan Project physicist who died days after a fatal radiation overdose from a criticality accident.)[52]

The explosion and fire threw hot particles of the nuclear fuel and also far more dangerous fission products, radioactive isotopes such as caesium-137, iodine-131, strontium-90 and other radionuclides, into the air: the residents of the surrounding area observed the radioactive cloud on the night of the explosion.

Equipment assembled included remote-controlled bulldozers and robot-carts that could detect radioactivity and carry hot debris. Valery Legasov (first deputy director of the Kurchatov Institute of Atomic Energy in Moscow) said, in 1987, "But we learned that robots are not the great remedy for everything. Where there was very high radiation, the robot ceased to be a robot—the electronics quit working."[53]

Timeline

- 1:26:03 – fire alarm activated
- 1:28 – arrival of local firefighters, Pravik's guard
- 1:35 – arrival of firefighters from Pripyat, Kibenok's guard
- 1:40 – arrival of Telyatnikov
- 2:10 – turbine hall roof fire extinguished
- 2:30 – main reactor hall roof fires suppressed
- 3:30 – arrival of Kiev firefighters[54]
- 4:50 – fires mostly localized
- 6:35 – all fires extinguished‡[55]

With the exception of the fire contained inside Reactor 4, which continued to burn for many days.[23]:73

Evacuation developments

The view of Chernobyl Nuclear Power Plant taken from the city of Pripyat evacuated after the incident. The townspeople went about their usual business, completely oblivious to what had just happened. However, within a few hours of the explosion, dozens of people fell ill. Later, they reported severe headaches and metallic tastes in their mouths, along with uncontrollable fits of coughing and vomiting.[56]

The general population of the Soviet Union was first informed of the disaster on 28 April, two days after the explosion, with a 20 second announcement in the TV news program _Vremya_.[57] At that time ABC released its report about the disaster.[58] During that time, all radio broadcasts run by the state were replaced with classical music, which was a common method of preparing the public for an announcement of a tragedy that had taken place. Scientist teams were armed and placed on alert as instructions were awaited.

Only after radiation levels set off alarms at the Forsmark Nuclear Power Plant in Sweden,[59] over one thousand kilometers from the Chernobyl Plant, did the Soviet Union admit that an accident had occurred. Nevertheless, authorities attempted to conceal the scale of the disaster.

For example, after evacuating the city of Pripyat, the following warning message was read on the state TV:

There has been an accident at the Chernobyl Nuclear Power Plant. One of the nuclear reactors was damaged. The effects of the accident are being remedied. Assistance has been provided for any affected people. An investigative commission has been set up.

—*Vremya*, 28 April 1986 (21:00)[57]

A state commission was set up the same day (26 April) and tasked with investigating the accident. It was headed by Valery Legasov, who arrived at Chernobyl in the evening of 26 April. By the time Legasov arrived, two people had already died and 52 were receiving medical attention in hospital. By the night of 26–27 April – more than 24 hours after the explosion – Legasov's committee had ample evidence that extremely high levels of radiation had caused a number of cases of radiation exposure. Based on the evidence at hand, Legasov's committee acknowledged the destruction of the reactor and ordered the evacuation of Pripyat.

The evacuation began at 14:00 on 27 April. An excerpt of the evacuation announcement was translated into English in the program *Seconds From Disaster* on the National Geographic Channel in 2004.[60] A translation of the rest of the audio follows.

For the attention of the residents of Pripyat! The City Council informs you that due to the accident at Chernobyl Power Station in the city of Pripyat the radioactive conditions in the vicinity are deteriorating. The Communist Party, its officials and the armed forces are taking necessary steps to combat this. Nevertheless, with the view to keep people as safe and healthy as possible, the children being top priority, we need to temporarily evacuate the citizens in the nearest towns of Kiev Oblast. For these reasons, starting from April 27, 1986 2 pm each apartment block will be able to have a bus at its disposal, supervised by the police and the city officials. It is highly advisable to take your documents, some vital personal belongings and a certain amount of food, just in case, with you. The senior executives of public and industrial facilities of the city has decided on the list of employees needed to stay in Pripyat to maintain these facilities in a good working order. All the houses will be guarded by the police during the evacuation period. Comrades, leaving your residences temporarily please make sure you have turned off the lights, electrical equipment and water and shut the windows. Please keep calm and orderly in the process of this short-term evacuation.

—Evacuation announcement in Pripyat, 27 April 1986 (14:00)

In order to expedite the evacuation, the residents were told to bring only what was necessary, as the authorities had said it would only last approximately three days. As a result, most of the residents left their personal belongings, which are still there today. An exclusion zone of 30 km (19 mi) remains in place today, although its shape has changed and its size has been expanded.

As the plant was run by authorities in Moscow, the government of Ukraine did not receive prompt information on the situation at the site, according to the former chairman of Presidium of Verkhovna Rada of Ukrainian SSR, Valentyna Shevchenko.[61] In her recollections she stated that she was at work when at 09:00 Vasyl Durdynets who performed duties of the Minister of Internal Affairs at the time (as the First Deputy Minister) called in with a report on the recent situation, adding at the end that there was a fire at the Chernobyl AES (AES – an abbreviation for a nuclear power plant), which was extinguished and everything was fine (see Fire containment). When Shevchenko asked "How are the people?", he replied that there was nothing to be concerned with: "some are celebrating a wedding, others are gardening, and others are fishing in the Pripyat River".[61]

On 25 April 2011 the President of Ukraine Viktor Yanukovych awarded Durdynets the "Distinguished Juror of Ukraine" as an advisor of the Ministry of Internal Affairs, a participant in the liquidation of consequences of Chernobyl disaster, and a general of Internal Service of Ukraine.[62] After the report Shevchenko called in to Volodymyr Shcherbytsky (Head of the Central Committee of the CPU, de facto head of state).[61] Shcherbytsky stated that he anticipated a delegation of the state commission headed by the deputy chairman of the Council of Ministers of USSR.[61]

Among the delegation's officials were academic Evgeny Velikhov, a leading nuclear specialist in the Soviet Union; a head of Hydro-Meteorologic Service of USSR Yuriy Izrael; a chief radiologist of the country Leonid Ilyin; and others. From the Boryspil International Airport the delegation drove to the power plant, realised the seriousness of the situation that night, and decided to evacuate the residents of Pripyat.[61] On 26 April 2011 Velikhov was awarded Order of Merit of the III degree from the President of Ukraine Viktor Yanukovych for his contributions in the liquidation of consequences of the Chernobyl disaster.[63]

By the morning of 27 April, buses arrived in Pripyat to start the evacuation at 11:00. By 15:00, 53,000 people were evacuated to various villages of Kiev region.[61] At first it was decided to evacuate the population temporarily for three days, however later it was postponed permanently. Many took only the most necessary items and their documents leaving all the rest behind.[61] The next day, talks began for evacuating people from the 10 km zone.

Shevchenko was the first of the Ukrainian state top officials to arrive at the disaster site early on 28 April. There she spoke with members of medical staff and people, who were calm and hopeful that they could soon return to their homes. Shevchenko returned home near midnight, stopping at a radiological checkpoint in Vilcha, one of the first that were set up soon after the accident.[61]

There was a notification from Moscow that there was no reason to postpone the 1 May celebrations (including the annual parade), but on 30 April a meeting of the Political bureau of the Central Committee of CP(b)U took place to discuss the plan for the upcoming celebration. Scientists were reporting that the radiological background in Kiev city was normal. At the meeting, which was finished at 18:00, it was decided to shorten celebrations from the regular 3.5–4 to under 2 hours.[61]

Steam explosion risk

Chernobyl <u>corium lava</u> flows formed by fuel-containing mass in the basement of the plant [64]

Two floors of bubbler pools beneath the reactor served as a large water reservoir for the emergency cooling pumps and as a pressure suppression system capable of condensing steam in case of a small broken steam pipe; the third floor above them, below the reactor, served as a steam tunnel. The steam released by a broken pipe was supposed to enter the steam tunnel and be led into the pools to bubble through a layer of water. After the disaster, the pools and the basement were flooded because of ruptured cooling water pipes and accumulated firefighting water, and constituted a serious steam explosion risk.

The <u>smoldering</u> graphite, fuel and other material above, at more than 1200 °C,[65] started to burn through the reactor floor and mixed with molten concrete from the reactor lining, creating <u>corium</u>, a radioactive semi-liquid material comparable to <u>lava</u>.[64][66] If this mixture had melted through the floor into the pool of water, it was feared it could have created a serious steam explosion that would have ejected more radioactive material from the reactor. It became necessary to drain the pool.[67]

The bubbler pool could be drained by opening its sluice gates. Volunteers in diving suits entered the radioactive water and managed to open the gates. These were the engineers Alexei Ananenko (who knew where the valves were) and Valeri Bezpalov, accompanied by a third man, Boris Baranov, who provided them with light from a lamp, though this lamp failed, leaving them to find the valves by feeling their way along a pipe. All of them returned to the surface and according to Ananenko, their colleagues jumped in joy when they heard they had managed to open the valves. Upon emerging from the water, the three were already suffering from radiation sickness and later died.[68] Some sources claim incorrectly that they died in the plant.[69]

It is likely that intense alpha radiation hydrolyzed the water, generating a low-pH hydrogen peroxide (H_2O_2) solution akin to an oxidizing acid.[70] Conversion of bubbler pool water to H_2O_2 is confirmed by the presence in the Chernobyl lavas of studtite and metastudtite,[71][72] the only minerals that contain peroxide.[73]

Fire brigade pumps were then used to drain the basement. The operation was not completed until 8 May, after 20,000 metric tons of highly radioactive water were pumped out.

With the bubbler pool gone, a meltdown was less likely to produce a powerful steam explosion. To do so, the molten core would now have to reach the water table below the reactor. To reduce the likelihood of this, it was decided to freeze the earth beneath the reactor, which would also stabilize the foundations. Using oil drilling equipment, the injection of liquid nitrogen began on 4 May. It was estimated that 25 metric tons of liquid nitrogen per day would be required to keep the soil frozen at −100 °C.[23]:59

This idea[74] was soon scrapped and the bottom room where the cooling system would have been installed was filled with concrete.

Debris removal

Chernobyl power plant in 2003 with the sarcophagus containment structure

The worst of the radioactive debris was collected inside what was left of the reactor, much of it shoveled in by liquidators wearing heavy protective gear (dubbed "bio-robots" by the military); these workers could only spend a maximum of 40 seconds at a time working on the rooftops of the surrounding buildings because of the extremely high doses of radiation given off by the blocks of graphite and other debris. The reactor itself was covered with bags of sand, lead and boric acid dropped from helicopters: some 5,000 metric tons of material were dropped during the week that followed the accident.

At the time there was still fear that the reactor could re-enter a self-sustaining nuclear chain-reaction and explode again, and a new containment structure was planned to prevent rain entering and triggering such an explosion, and to prevent further release of radioactive material. This was the largest civil engineering task in history, involving a quarter of a million construction workers who all reached their official lifetime limits of radiation.[51] By December 1986, a large concrete sarcophagus had been erected to seal off the reactor and its contents.[75] A unique "clean up" medal was given to the workers.[76]

Many of the vehicles used by the "liquidators" remain parked in a field in the Chernobyl area.[77]

During the construction of the sarcophagus, a scientific team re-entered the reactor as part of an investigation dubbed "Complex Expedition", to locate and contain nuclear fuel in a way that could not lead to another explosion. These scientists manually collected cold fuel rods, but great heat was still emanating from the core. Rates of radiation in different parts of the building were monitored by drilling holes into the reactor and inserting long metal detector tubes. The scientists were exposed to high levels of radiation and radioactive dust.[51]

After six months of investigation, in December 1986, they discovered with the help of a remote camera an intensely radioactive mass in the basement of Unit Four, more than two meters wide and weighing hundreds of tons, which they called "the elephant's foot" for its wrinkled appearance. The mass was composed of sand, glass and a large amount of nuclear fuel that had escaped from the reactor. The concrete beneath the reactor was steaming hot, and was breached by solidified lava and spectacular unknown crystalline forms termed chernobylite. It was concluded that there was no further risk of explosion.[51]

Causes

There were two official explanations of the accident.

Operator error

The first official explanation of the accident, later acknowledged to be erroneous, was published in August 1986. It effectively placed the blame on the power plant operators. To investigate the causes of the accident the IAEA created a group known as the International Nuclear Safety Advisory Group (INSAG), which in its report of 1986, INSAG-1, on the whole also supported this view, based on the data provided by the Soviets and the oral statements of specialists.[78] In this view, the catastrophic accident was caused by gross violations of operating rules and regulations. "During preparation and testing of the turbine generator under run-down conditions using the auxiliary load, personnel disconnected a series of technical protection systems and breached the most important operational safety provisions for conducting a technical exercise."[79]:311

The operator error was probably due to their lack of knowledge of nuclear reactor physics and engineering, as well as lack of experience and training. According to these allegations, at the time of the accident the reactor was being operated with many key safety systems turned off, most notably the Emergency Core Cooling System (ECCS), LAR (Local Automatic control system), and AZ (emergency power reduction system). Personnel had an insufficiently detailed understanding of technical procedures involved with the nuclear reactor, and knowingly ignored regulations to speed test completion.[79]

40

The developers of the reactor plant considered this combination of events to be impossible and therefore did not allow for the creation of emergency protection systems capable of preventing the combination of events that led to the crisis, namely the intentional disabling of emergency protection equipment plus the violation of operating procedures. Thus the primary cause of the accident was the extremely improbable combination of rule infringement plus the operational routine allowed by the power station staff.[79]:312

In this analysis of the causes of the accident, deficiencies in the reactor design and in the operating regulations that made the accident possible were set aside and mentioned only casually. Serious critical observations covered only general questions and did not address the specific reasons for the accident. The following general picture arose from these observations. Several procedural irregularities also helped to make the accident possible. One was insufficient communication between the safety officers and the operators in charge of the experiment being run that night.

The reactor operators disabled safety systems down to the generators, which the test was really about. The main process computer, SKALA, was running in such a way that the main control computer could not shut down the reactor or even reduce power. Normally the reactor would have started to insert all of the control rods. The computer would have also started the "Emergency Core Protection System" that introduces 24 control rods into the active zone within 2.5 seconds, which is still slow by 1986 standards. All control was transferred from the process computer to the human operators.

On the subject of the disconnection of safety systems, Valery Legasov said, in 1987, "It was like airplane pilots experimenting with the engines in flight."[53]

This view is reflected in numerous publications and also artistic works on the theme of the Chernobyl accident that appeared immediately after the accident,[23] and for a long time remained dominant in the public consciousness and in popular publications.

Operating instructions and design deficiencies found

Reactor hall No. 1, Chernobyl nuclear power plant, Ukraine

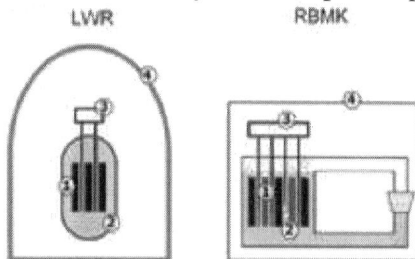

A simplified diagram of the major differences between the Chernobyl RBMK and the most common nuclear reactor design, the Light water reactor. 1. The use of a graphite moderator in a water cooled reactor. 2. A positive steam void coefficient that made the power excursion possible, which blew the reactor vessel. 3. The control rods were very slow, taking 18-20 seconds to be deployed. With the control rods having graphite tips that moderated, and therefore increased the fission rate in the beginning of the rod insertion 4. No reinforced containment building.[80][81][82]

Lumps of graphite moderator ejected from the core. The largest lump shows an intact control rod channel.

In 1991 a Commission of the USSR State Committee for the Supervision of Safety in Industry and Nuclear Power has reassessed the causes and circumstances of the Chernobyl accident and came to new insights and conclusions. Based on it, in 1992 the IAEA Nuclear Safety Advisory Group (INSAG) published an additional report, INSAG-7,[27] which reviewed "that part of the INSAG-1 report in which primary attention is given to the reasons for the accident" and included the USSR State Commission report as Appendix I.[27]

In this INSAG report, most of the earlier accusations against staff for breach of regulations were acknowledged to be either erroneous, based on incorrect information obtained in August 1986, or less relevant. This report reflected another view of the main reasons for the accident, presented in Appendix I. According to this account, the operators' actions in turning off the Emergency Core Cooling System, interfering with the settings on the protection equipment, and blocking the level and pressure in the separator drum did not contribute to the original cause of the accident and its magnitude, although they may have been a breach of regulations. Turning off the emergency system designed to prevent the two turbine generators from stopping was not a violation of regulations.[27]

Human factors contributed to the conditions that led to the disaster. These included operating the reactor at a low power level – less than 700 MW – a level documented in the run-down test program, and operating with a small operational reactivity margin (ORM). The 1986 assertions of Soviet experts notwithstanding, regulations did not prohibit operating the reactor at this low power level.[27]:18

However, regulations did forbid operating the reactor with a small margin of reactivity. Yet "post-accident studies have shown that the way in which the real role of the ORM is reflected in the Operating Procedures and design documentation for the RBMK-1000 is extremely contradictory," and furthermore, "ORM was not treated as an operational safety limit, violation of which could lead to an accident."[27]:34–25

According to the INSAG-7 Report, the chief reasons for the accident lie in the peculiarities of physics and in the construction of the reactor. There are two such reasons:[27]:18

- The reactor had a dangerously large positive void coefficient of reactivity. The void coefficient is a measurement of how a reactor responds to increased steam formation in the water coolant. Most other reactor designs have a negative coefficient, i.e. the nuclear reaction rate slows when steam bubbles form in the coolant, since as the vapor phase in the reactor increases, fewer neutrons are slowed down. Faster neutrons are less likely to split uranium atoms, so the reactor produces less power (a negative feed-back). Chernobyl's RBMK reactor, however, used solid graphite as a neutron moderator to slow down the neutrons, and the water in it, on the contrary, acts like a harmful neutron absorber. Thus neutrons are slowed down even if steam bubbles form in the water. Furthermore, because steam absorbs neutrons much less readily than water, increasing the intensity of vaporization means that more neutrons are able to split uranium atoms, increasing the reactors power output. This makes the RBMK design very unstable at low power levels, and prone to suddenly increasing energy production to a dangerous level. This behavior is counter-intuitive, and this property of the reactor was unknown to the crew.
- A more significant flaw was in the design of the control rods that are inserted into the reactor to slow down the reaction. In the RBMK reactor design, the lower part of each control rod was made of graphite and was 1.3 meters shorter than necessary, and in the space beneath the rods were hollow channels filled with water. The upper part of the rod, the truly functional part that absorbs the neutrons and

45

thereby halts the reaction, was made of <u>boron carbide</u>. With this design, when the rods are inserted into the reactor from the uppermost position, the graphite parts initially displace some water (which absorbs neutrons, as mentioned above), effectively causing less neutrons to be absorbed initially. Thus for the first few seconds of control rod activation, reactor power output is increased, rather than reduced as desired. This behavior is counter-intuitive and was not known to the reactor operators.

- Other deficiencies besides these were noted in the RBMK-1000 reactor design, as were its non-compliance with accepted standards and with the requirements of nuclear reactor safety.

Analysis of views

Both views were heavily lobbied by different groups, including the reactor's designers, power plant personnel, and the Soviet and Ukrainian governments. According to the IAEA's 1986 analysis, the main cause of the accident was the operators' actions. But according to the IAEA's 1993 revised analysis the main cause was the reactor's design.[83] One reason there were such contradictory viewpoints and so much debate about the causes of the Chernobyl accident was that the primary data covering the disaster, as registered by the instruments and sensors, were not completely published in the official sources.

Once again, the human factor had to be considered as a major element in causing the accident. INSAG notes that both the operating regulations and staff handled the disabling of the reactor protection easily enough: witness the length of time for which the ECCS was out of service while the reactor was operated at half power. INSAG's view is that it was the operating crew's deviation from the test program that was mostly to blame. "Most reprehensibly, unapproved changes in the test procedure were deliberately made on the spot, although the plant was known to be in a very different condition from that intended for the test."[27]:24

As in the previously released report INSAG-1, close attention is paid in report INSAG-7 to the inadequate (at the moment of the accident) "culture of safety" at all levels. Deficiency in the safety culture was inherent not only at the operational stage but also, and to no lesser extent, during activities at other stages in the lifetime of nuclear power plants (including design, engineering, construction, manufacture and regulation). The poor quality of operating procedures and instructions, and their conflicting character, put a heavy burden on the operating crew, including the Chief Engineer. "The accident can be said to have flowed from a deficient safety culture, not only at the Chernobyl plant, but throughout the Soviet design, operating and regulatory organizations for nuclear power that existed at that time."[27]:24

Effects

National and international spread of radioactive substances

Four hundred times more radioactive material was released from Chernobyl than by the atomic bombing of Hiroshima. The disaster released 1/100 to 1/1000 of the total amount of radioactivity released by nuclear weapons testing during the 1950s and 1960s.[84] Approximately 100,000 km² of land was significantly contaminated with fallout, with the worst hit regions being in Belarus, Ukraine and Russia.[85] Slighter levels of contamination were detected over all of Europe except for the Iberian Peninsula.[17][86][87]

The initial evidence that a major release of radioactive material was affecting other countries came not from Soviet sources, but from Sweden. On the morning of 28 April[88] workers at the Forsmark Nuclear Power Plant (approximately 1,100 km (680 mi) from the Chernobyl site) were found to have radioactive particles on their clothes.[89]

It was Sweden's search for the source of radioactivity, after they had determined there was no leak at the Swedish plant that at noon on 28 April led to the first hint of a serious nuclear problem in the western Soviet Union. Hence the evacuation of Pripyat on 27 April 36 hours after the initial explosions, was silently completed before the disaster became known outside the Soviet Union. The rise in radiation levels had at that time already been measured in Finland, but a civil service strike delayed the response and publication.[90]

Areas of Europe contaminated with ^{137}Cs[91]

Country	37–185 k Bq/m²		185–555 kBq/m²		555–1480 kBq/m²		>1480 kBq/m²	
	km²	% of country	km²	% of country	km²	% of country	km²	% of country
Belarus	29,900	14.4	10,200	4.9	4,200	2.0	2,200	1.1
Ukraine	37,200	6.2	3,200	0.53	900	0.15	600	0.1
Russia	49,800	0.29	5,700	0.03	2,100	0.01	300	0.002
Sweden	12,000	2.7	—	—	—	—	—	—
Finland	11,500	3.4	—	—	—	—	—	—
Austria	8,600	10.3	—	—	—	—	—	—
Norway	5,200	1.3	—	—	—	—	—	—
Bulgaria	4,800	4.3	—	—	—	—	—	—
Switzerland	1,300	3.1	—	—	—	—	—	—
Greece	1,200	0.91	—	—	—	—	—	—
Slovenia	300	1.5	—	—	—	—	—	—
Italy	300	0.1	—	—	—	—	—	—
Moldova	60	0.2	—	—	—	—	—	—
Totals	162,160 km²		19,100 km²		7,200 km²		3,100 km²	

Contamination from the Chernobyl accident was scattered irregularly depending on weather conditions, much of it deposited on mountainous regions such as the Alps, the Welsh mountains and the Scottish Highlands, where adiabatic cooling caused radioactive rainfall. The resulting patches of contamination were often highly localized, and water-flows across the ground contributed further to large variations in radioactivity over small areas. Sweden and Norway also received heavy fallout when the contaminated air collided with a cold front, bringing rain.[92]:43–44, 78

Rain was purposely seeded over 10,000 km^2 of the Belorussian SSR by the Soviet air force to remove radioactive particles from clouds heading toward highly populated areas. Heavy, black-colored rain fell on the city of Gomel.[93] Reports from Soviet and Western scientists indicate that Belarus received about 60% of the contamination that fell on the former Soviet Union. However, the 2006 TORCH report stated that half of the volatile particles had landed outside Ukraine, Belarus, and Russia. A large area in Russia south of Bryansk was also contaminated, as were parts of northwestern Ukraine. Studies in surrounding countries indicate that over one million people could have been affected by radiation.[94]

Recently published data from a long-term monitoring program (The Korma Report)[95] shows a decrease in internal radiation exposure of the inhabitants of a region in Belarus close to Gomel. Resettlement may even be possible in prohibited areas provided that people comply with appropriate dietary rules.

In Western Europe, precautionary measures taken in response to the radiation included seemingly arbitrary regulations banning the importation of certain foods but not others. In France some officials stated that the Chernobyl accident had no adverse effects.[96] Official figures in southern Bavaria in Germany indicated that some wild plant species contained substantial levels of cesium, which were believed to have been passed onto them by wild boars, a significant number of which had already contained

51

radioactive particles above the allowed level, consuming them.[*clarification needed*][97]

Piglet with dipygus on exhibit at the Ukrainian National Chornobyl Museum.

Mutations in both humans and other animals increased following the disaster. On farms in Narodychi Raion of Ukraine, for instance, in the first four years of the disaster nearly 350 animals were born with gross deformities such as missing or extra limbs, missing eyes, heads or ribs, or deformed skulls; in comparison, only three abnormal births had been registered in the five years prior.[98][99][100][101][102][103] Despite these claims, the World Health Organization states, "children conceived before or after their father's exposure showed no statistically significant differences in mutation frequencies."[104]

Radioactive release

Like many other releases of radioactivity into the environment, the Chernobyl release was controlled by the physical and chemical properties of the radioactive elements in the core. Particularly dangerous are the highly radioactive fission products, those with high nuclear decay rates that accumulate in the food chain, such as some of the isotopes of iodine, cesium and strontium. Iodine-131 and caesium-137 are responsible for most of the radiation exposure received by the general population.[105]

Two reports on the release of radioisotopes from the site were made available, one by the OSTI and a more detailed report by the OECD, both in 1998.[106][107] At different times after the accident, different isotopes were responsible for the majority of the external dose.

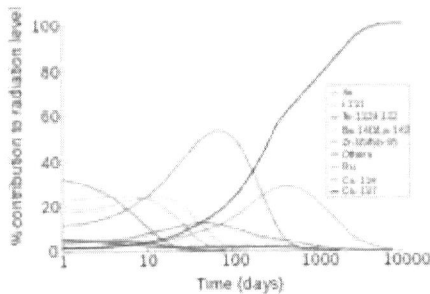

Contributions of the various isotopes to the external (atmospheric) absorbed dose in the contaminated area of Pripyat, from soon after the accident, to years after the accident.

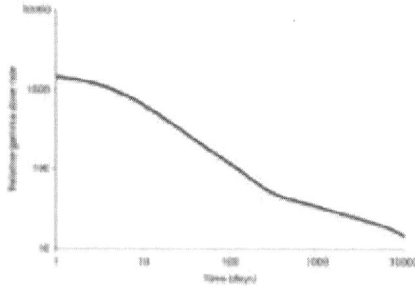

The external relative gamma dose for a person in the open near the Chernobyl disaster site.

The release of radioisotopes from the nuclear fuel was largely controlled by their boiling points, and the majority of the radioactivity present in the core was retained in the reactor.

- All of the noble gases, including krypton and xenon, contained within the reactor were released immediately into the atmosphere by the first steam explosion.[105]
- 50 to 60% of all core radio-iodine in the reactor, containing about 1760 PBq (1760×10^{15} becquerels), which in mass units is 0.4 kg of iodine-131, was released, as a mixture of sublimed vapor, solid particles, and organic iodine compounds. Half-life 8 days.[105] The activity of any radioisotope, and therefore the quantity of that isotope remaining, after 7 decay half lifes have passed, is less than 1% of its initial magnitude,[108] and it continues to reduce beyond 0.78% after 7 half lifes to 0.098% remaining after 10 half lifes have passed and so on.[109][110]
- 20 to 40% of all core caesium-137 was released, 85 PBq in all.[105][111] Caesium was released in aerosol form; caesium-137, along with isotopes of

strontium, are the two primary elements preventing the Chernobyl exclusion zone being re-inhabited.[112] The caesium-137 activity represented by 8.5×10^{16} Bq, would be produced by 24 kilograms of caesium-137.[112] Cs-137 has a half-life of 30 years.[105]

- Tellurium-132, half-life 78 hours, an estimated 1150 PBq was released.[105]
- Xenon-133, the total radioactivity atmospheric release is estimated at 5200 PBq, Xe-133 has a half-life of 5 days.[105]
- An early estimate for total nuclear fuel material released to the environment was 3 ± 1.5%; this was later revised to 3.5 ± 0.5%. This corresponds to the atmospheric emission of 6 t of fragmented fuel.[107]

Two sizes of particles were released: small particles of 0.3 to 1.5 micrometers (aerodynamic diameter) and large particles of 10 micrometers. The large particles contained about 80% to 90% of the released nonvolatile radioisotopes zirconium-95, niobium-95, lanthanum-140, cerium-144 and the transuranic elements, including neptunium, plutonium and the minor actinides, embedded in a uranium oxide matrix.

The dose that was calculated is the relative external gamma dose rate for a person standing in the open. The exact dose to a person in the real world who would spend most of their time sleeping indoors in a shelter and then venturing out to consume an internal dose from the inhalation or ingestion of a radioisotope, requires a personnel specific radiation dose reconstruction analysis.

Health of plant workers and local people

In the aftermath of the accident, 237 people suffered from acute radiation sickness (ARS), of whom 31 died within the first three months.[13][113] Most of the victims were fire and rescue workers trying to bring the accident under control, who were not fully aware of how dangerous the exposure to radiation in the smoke was. Whereas, in the World Health Organization's 2006 report of the Chernobyl Forum expert group on the 237 emergency workers who were diagnosed with ARS, ARS was identified as the cause of death for 28 of these people within the first few months after the disaster.

No further ARS-related deaths were identified in the general population affected by the disaster. Of the 72,000 Russian Emergency Workers being studied, 216 non-cancer deaths are attributed to the disaster, between 1991 and 1998.[citation needed] Of all 66,000 Belarusian emergency workers, by the mid-1990s only 150 (roughly 0.2%) were reported by their government as having died. In contrast, 5,722 casualties were reported among Ukrainian clean-up workers up to the year 1995, by the National Committee for Radiation Protection of the Ukrainian Population.[85]

The latency period for solid cancers caused by excess radiation exposure is 10 or more years; thus at the time of the WHO report being undertaken, the rates of solid cancer deaths were no greater than the general population.[citation needed][dubious – discuss] Some 135,000 people were evacuated from the area, including 50,000 from Pripyat.

Residual radioactivity in the environment

Rivers, lakes and reservoirs

Earth Observing-1 image of the reactor and surrounding area in April 2009

The Chernobyl nuclear power plant is located next to the Pripyat River, which feeds into the Dnieper reservoir system, one of the largest surface water systems in Europe, which at the time supplied water to Kiev's 2.4 million residents, and was still in spring flood when the accident occurred.[114]:60 The radioactive contamination of aquatic systems therefore became a major problem in the immediate aftermath of the accident.[115] In the most affected areas of Ukraine, levels of radioactivity (particularly from radionuclides ^{131}I, ^{137}Cs and ^{90}Sr) in drinking water caused concern during the weeks and months after the accident,[115] though officially it was stated that all contaminants had settled to the bottom "in an insoluble phase" and would not dissolve for 800–1,000 years.[114]:64 Guidelines for levels of radioiodine in drinking water were temporarily raised to 3,700 Bq/L, allowing most water to be reported as safe,[115] and a year after the accident it was announced that even the water of the

Chernobyl plant's cooling pond was within acceptable norms. Despite this, two months after the disaster the Kiev water supply was abruptly switched from the Dnieper to the Desna River.[114]:64–5 Meanwhile, massive silt traps were constructed, along with an enormous 30m-deep underground barrier to prevent groundwater from the destroyed reactor entering the Pripyat River.[114]:65–7

Bio-accumulation of radioactivity in fish[116] resulted in concentrations (both in western Europe and in the former Soviet Union) that in many cases were significantly above guideline maximum levels for consumption.[115] Guideline maximum levels for radiocaesium in fish vary from country to country but are approximately 1,000 Bq/kg in the European Union.[117] In the Kiev Reservoir in Ukraine, concentrations in fish were several thousand Bq/kg during the years after the accident.[116]

In small "closed" lakes in Belarus and the Bryansk region of Russia, concentrations in a number of fish species varied from 100 to 60,000 Bq/kg during the period 1990–92.[118] The contamination of fish caused short-term concern in parts of the UK and Germany and in the long term (years rather than months) in the affected areas of Ukraine, Belarus, and Russia as well as in parts of Scandinavia.[115]

Groundwater

Map of radiation levels in 1996 around Chernobyl

Groundwater was not badly affected by the Chernobyl accident since radionuclides with short half-lives decayed away long before they could affect groundwater supplies, and longer-lived radionuclides such as radiocaesium and radiostrontium were adsorbed to surface soils before they could transfer to groundwater.[119] However, significant transfers of radionuclides to groundwater have occurred from waste disposal sites in the 30 km (19 mi) exclusion zone around Chernobyl. Although there is a potential for transfer of radionuclides from these disposal sites off-site (i.e. out of the 30 km (19 mi) exclusion zone), the IAEA

Chernobyl Report [119] argues that this is not significant in comparison to current levels of washout of surface-deposited radioactivity.

Flora and fauna

After the disaster, four square kilometers of pine forest directly downwind of the reactor turned reddish-brown and died, earning the name of the "Red Forest".[120]

After the disaster, four square kilometers of pine forest directly downwind of the reactor turned reddish-brown and died, earning the name of the "Red Forest".[120] Some animals in the worst-hit areas also died or stopped reproducing. Most domestic animals were removed from the exclusion zone, but horses left on an island in the Pripyat River 6 km (4 mi) from the power plant died when their thyroid glands were destroyed by radiation doses of 150–200 Sv.[121] Some cattle on the same island died and those that survived were stunted because of thyroid damage. The next generation appeared to be normal.[121]

A robot sent into the reactor itself has returned with samples of black, melanin-rich radiotrophic fungi that are growing on the reactor's walls.[122]

Of the 440,350 wild boar killed in the 2010 hunting season in Germany, over 1,000 were found to be contaminated with levels of radiation above the permitted limit of 600 bequerels per kilogram, due to residual radioactivity from Chernobyl.[123] Germany has "banned wild game meat because of contamination linked to radioactive mushrooms".[124]

The Norwegian Agricultural Authority reported that in 2009 a total of 18,000 livestock in Norway needed to be given uncontaminated feed for a period of time before slaughter in order to ensure that their meat was safe for human consumption. This was due to residual radioactivity from Chernobyl in the plants they graze on in the wild during the summer. 1,914 sheep needed to be given uncontaminated feed for a period of time before slaughter during 2012, and these sheep were located in just 18 of Norway's municipalities, a decrease of 17 from the 35 municipalities affected animals were located in during 2011 (117 municipalities were affected during 1986).[125]

The after-effects of Chernobyl were expected to be seen for a further 100 years, although the severity of the effects would decline over that period.[126] Scientists report this is due to radioactive caesium-137 isotopes being taken up by fungi such as *Cortinarius caperatus* which is in turn eaten by sheep whilst grazing.[125]

The United Kingdom was forced to restrict the movement of sheep from upland areas when radioactive caesium-137 fell across parts of Northern Ireland, Wales, Scotland and northern England. In the immediate aftermath of the disaster in 1986, a total of 4,225,000 sheep had their movement restricted across a total of 9,700 farms, in order to prevent contaminated meat entering the human food chain.[127] The number of sheep and the number of farms affected has decreased since 1986, Northern Ireland was released from all restrictions in 2000 and by 2009 369 farms containing around 190,000 sheep remained under the restrictions in Wales, Cumbria and northern Scotland.[127] The restrictions applying in Scotland were lifted in 2010, whilst those applying to Wales and Cumbria were lifted during 2012, meaning no farms in the UK remain restricted because of Chernobyl fallout.[128][129]

The legislation used to control sheep movement and compensate farmers (farmers were latterly compensated £1.30 per animal to cover additional costs in holding animals prior to radiation monitoring) was revoked during October and November 2012 by the relevant authorities in the UK.[130]

Human impact

Chernobyl disaster effects

Demonstration on Chernobyl day near <u>WHO</u> in Geneva

The Chernobyl Forum first met on 3 February 2003 for a three-day meeting. It consisted of the International Atomic Energy Agency (IAEA), other United Nations organizations (FAO, UN-OCHA, UNDP, UNEP, UNSCEAR, WHO, and the <u>World Bank</u>), and the governments of Belarus, Russia, and Ukraine. A second meeting was held on 10–11 March 2004, and a third on 18–20 April 2005. The aim of the Forum was to "scientifically clarify the radiological environmental and health consequences of the Chernobyl accident, to provide advice on and to contribute to a scientifically sound remediation and health care programmes, and to consider the necessity of, and opportunities for continued research/learning lessons."[131] A report was published by Chernobyl Forum in 2005.

On the death toll of the accident, the report states that twenty-eight emergency workers ("liquidators") died from <u>acute radiation syndrome</u> including <u>beta burns</u> and 15 patients died from thyroid cancer in the following years,

63

and it roughly estimated that cancer deaths caused by Chernobyl may reach a total of about 4,000 among the 5 million persons residing in the contaminated areas, the report projected cancer mortality "increases of less than one per cent" (~0.3%) on a time span of 80 years, cautioning that this estimate was "speculative" since at this time only a few cancer deaths are linked to the Chernobyl disaster.[132] The report says it is impossible to reliably predict the number of fatal cancers arising from the incident as small differences in assumptions can result in large differences in the estimated health costs. The report says it represents the consensus view of the eight UN organisations.

Thyroid cancer

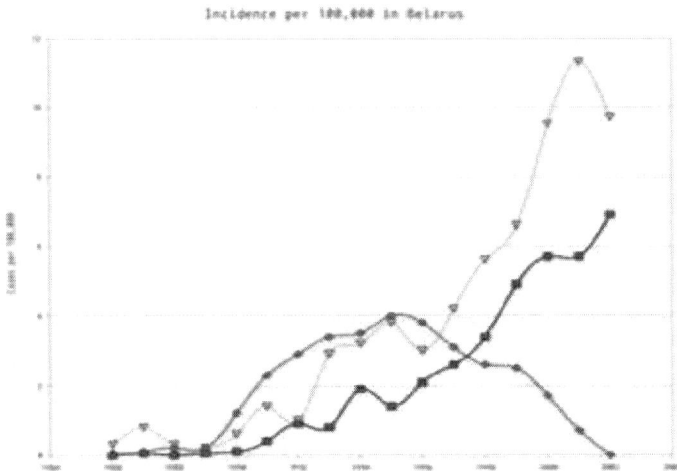

Thyroid cancer incidence in children and adolescents from Belarus after the Chernobyl accident
Yellow: Adults (19–34)
Blue: Adolescents (15–18)
Red: Children (0–14)

The 2005 Chernobyl Forum report revealed thyroid cancer among children to be one of the main health impacts from the Chernobyl accident. In that publication more than 4000 cases were reported, and that there was no evidence of an increase in solid cancers or leukemia. It said that there was an increase in psychological problems among the affected population.[132] Dr Michael Repacholi, manager of WHO's Radiation Program reported that the 4000 cases of thyroid cancer resulted in nine deaths.[133]

According to UNSCEAR, up to the year 2005, an excess of over 6000 cases of thyroid cancer have been reported. That is, over the estimated pre-accident baseline thyroid cancer rate, more than 6000 casual cases of thyroid cancer have been reported in children and adolescents exposed at the time of the accident, a number that is expected to increase. They concluded that there is no other evidence of major health impacts from the radiation exposure.[134]

Well-differentiated thyroid cancers are generally treatable,[135] and when treated the five-year survival rate of thyroid cancer is 96%, and 92% after 30 years.[136] UNSCEAR had reported 15 deaths from thyroid cancer in 2011.[137] The International Atomic Energy Agency (IAEA) also states that there has been no increase in the rate of birth defects or abnormalities, or solid cancers (such as lung cancer) corroborating UNSCEAR's assessments.[138] UNSCEAR does raise the possibility of long term genetic defects, pointing to a doubling of radiation-induced minisatellite mutations among children born in 1994.[139] However, the risk of thyroid cancer associated with the Chernobyl accident is still high according to published studies.[140][141]

The German affiliate of the International Physicians for the Prevention of Nuclear War (IPPNW) argued that more than

10,000 people are today affected by thyroid cancer and 50,000 cases are expected in the future.[142]

Other health disorders

Fred Mettler, a radiation expert at the University of New Mexico, puts the number of worldwide cancer deaths outside the highly contaminated zone at "perhaps" 5000, for a total of 9000 Chernobyl-associated fatal cancers, saying "the number is small (representing a few percent) relative to the normal spontaneous risk of cancer, but the numbers are large in absolute terms".[143] The same report outlined studies based in data found in the Russian Registry from 1991 to 1998 that suggested that "of 61,000 Russian workers exposed to an average dose of 107 mSv about 5% of all fatalities that occurred may have been due to radiation exposure."[132]

The report went into depth about the risks to mental health of exaggerated fears about the effects of radiation.[132] According to the IAEA the "designation of the affected population as "victims" rather than "survivors" has led them to perceive themselves as helpless, weak and lacking control over their future". The IAEA says that this may have led to behavior that has caused further health effects.[144]

Fred Mettler commented that 20 years later "The population remains largely unsure of what the effects of radiation actually are and retain a sense of foreboding. A number of adolescents and young adults who have been exposed to modest or small amounts of radiation feel that they are somehow fatally flawed and there is no downside to using illicit drugs or having unprotected sex. To reverse such attitudes and behaviors will likely take years although some youth groups have begun programs that have

66

promise."[145] In addition, disadvantaged children around Chernobyl suffer from health problems that are attributable not only to the Chernobyl accident, but also to the poor state of post-Soviet health systems.[138]

The United Nations Scientific Committee on the Effects of Atomic Radiation (UNSCEAR), part of the Chernobyl Forum, have produced their own assessments of the radiation effects.[146] UNSCEAR was set up as a collaboration between various United Nation bodies, including the World Health Organization, after the atomic bomb attacks on Hiroshima and Nagasaki, to assess the long-term effects of radiation on human health.[147]

Deaths due to radiation exposure

The number of potential deaths arising from the Chernobyl disaster is heavily debated. The WHO's prediction of 4,000 future cancer deaths in surrounding countries[148] is based on the Linear no-threshold model (LNT), which assumes that the damage inflicted by radiation at low doses is directly proportional to the dose.[149] Radiation epidemiologist Roy Shore contends that estimating health effects in a population from the LNT model "is not wise because of the uncertainties".[150]

Radiation warning sign in Pripyat

According to the Union of Concerned Scientists the number of excess cancer deaths worldwide (including all contaminated areas) is approximately 27,000 based on the same LNT.[151]

Another study critical of the Chernobyl Forum report was commissioned by Greenpeace, which asserted that the most recently published figures indicate that in Belarus, Russia and Ukraine the accident could have resulted in 10,000-200,000 additional deaths in the period between 1990 and 2004.[152] The Scientific Secretary of the Chernobyl Forum criticized the report's reliance on non-peer reviewed locally produced studies. Although most of the study's sources were from peer-reviewed journals, including many Western medical journals, the higher mortality estimates were from non-peer-reviewed sources[152]), while Gregory Härtl (spokesman for the WHO) suggested that the conclusions were motivated by ideology.[153]

Chernobyl: Consequences of the Catastrophe for People and the Environment is an English translation of the 2007 Russian publication *Chernobyl*. It was published in 2009 by the New York Academy of Sciences in their *Annals of the New York Academy of Sciences*. It presents an analysis of scientific literature and concludes that medical records between 1986, the year of the accident, and 2004 reflect 985,000 premature deaths as a result of the radioactivity released.[154] Though, it was impossible to precisely determine what dose the affected people received, knowing the fact that the received doses varied strongly from one individual to the other in the population above which the radioactive cloud travelled, and also knowing the fact that one cannot tell for sure if a cancer in an individual from the former USSR is produced by radiation from Chernobyl accident or by other social or behavioral factors, such as smoking or alcohol drinking.[155]

The authors suggest that most of the deaths were in Russia, Belarus and Ukraine, though others occurred worldwide throughout the many countries that were struck by radioactive fallout from Chernobyl. The literature analysis draws on over 1,000 published titles and over 5,000 internet and printed publications discussing the consequences of the Chernobyl disaster. The authors contend that those publications and papers were written by leading Eastern European authorities and have largely been downplayed or ignored by the IAEA and UNSCEAR.[154] This estimate has however been criticized as exaggerated, lacking a proper scientific base.[22]

Abortion requests

Following the accident, journalists mistrusted many medical professionals (such as the spokesman from the UK National Radiological Protection Board), and in turn encouraged the public to mistrust them.[156] Throughout the European continent, in nations where abortion is legal, many requests for induced abortions, of otherwise normal pregnancies, were obtained out of fears of radiation from Chernobyl; including an excess number of abortions in Denmark in the months following the accident.[157] In Greece, following the accident many obstetricians were unable to resist requests from worried pregnant mothers over fears of radiation. Although it was determined that the effective dose to Greeks would not exceed 1 mSv (100 mrem), a dose much lower than that which could induce embryonic abnormalities or other non-stochastic effects, there was an observed 2500 excess of otherwise wanted pregnancies being terminated, probably out of fear in the mother of radiation risk.[158] A "slightly" above the expected number of requested induced abortions occurred in Italy.[159][160]

Other conditions

According to Kenneth Mossman, a Professor of Health Physics and member of the U.S. Nuclear Regulatory Commission advisory committee,[161] the "LNT philosophy is overly conservative, and low-level radiation may be less dangerous than commonly believed".[162] Yoshihisa Matsumoto, a radiation biologist at the Tokyo Institute of Technology, cites laboratory experiments on animals to suggest there must be a threshold dose below which DNA repair mechanisms can completely repair any radiation damage.[150] Mossman suggests that the proponents of the current model believe that being conservative is justified due to the uncertainties surrounding low level doses and it is better to have a "prudent public health policy".[161]

Another significant issue is establishing consistent data on which to base the analysis of the impact of the Chernobyl accident. Since 1991 large social and political changes have occurred within the affected regions and these changes have had significant impact on the administration of health care, on socio-economic stability, and the manner in which statistical data is collected.[163] Ronald Chesser, a radiation biologist at Texas Tech University, says that "the subsequent Soviet collapse, scarce funding, imprecise dosimetry, and difficulties tracking people over the years have limited the number of studies and their reliability."[150]

Economic and political consequences

It is difficult to establish the total economic cost of the disaster. According to Mikhail Gorbachev, the Soviet Union spent 18 billion rubles (the equivalent of US$18 billion at that time) on containment and decontamination, virtually bankrupting itself.[2] In Belarus the total cost over 30 years is estimated at US$235 billion (in 2005 dollars).[138] On-going costs are well known; in their 2003–2005 report, The Chernobyl Forum stated that between 5% and 7% of government spending in Ukraine is still related to Chernobyl, while in Belarus over $13 billion is thought to have been spent between 1991 and 2003, with 22% of national budget having been Chernobyl-related in 1991, falling to 6% by 2002.[138] Much of the current cost relates to the payment of Chernobyl-related social benefits to some 7 million people across the 3 countries.[138]

A significant economic impact at the time was the removal of 784,320 ha (1,938,100 acres) of agricultural land and 694,200 ha (1,715,000 acres) of forest from production. While much of this has been returned to use, agricultural production costs have risen due to the need for special cultivation techniques, fertilizers and additives.[138]

Politically, the accident gave great significance to the new Soviet policy of glasnost,[164][165] and helped forge closer Soviet-US relations at the end of the Cold War, through bioscientific cooperation.[166]:44–48 But the disaster also became a key factor in the Union's eventual 1991 dissolution, and a major influence in shaping the new Eastern Europe.[166]:20–21

Aftermath

Following the accident, questions arose about the future of the plant and its eventual fate. All work on the unfinished reactors 5 and 6 was halted three years later. However, the trouble at the Chernobyl plant did not end with the disaster in reactor 4. The damaged reactor was sealed off and 200 cubic meters (260 cu yd) of concrete was placed between the disaster site and the operational buildings.[*citation needed*] The Ukrainian government continued to let the three remaining reactors operate because of an energy shortage in the country.

Decommissioning

Main article: Chernobyl Nuclear Power Plant Decommissioning

In 1991, a fire broke out in the turbine building of reactor 2;[167] the authorities subsequently declared the reactor damaged beyond repair and had it taken offline. Reactor 1 was decommissioned in November 1996 as part of a deal between the Ukrainian government and international organizations such as the IAEA to end operations at the plant. On 15 December 2000, then-President Leonid Kuchma personally turned off Reactor 3 in an official ceremony, shutting down the entire site.[168]

Radioactive waste management

Containment of the reactor

The Chernobyl reactor is now enclosed in a large concrete sarcophagus, which was built quickly to allow continuing operation of the other reactors at the plant.[169]

A New Safe Confinement was to have been built by the end of 2005; however, it has suffered ongoing delays and as of 2010, when construction finally began, was expected to be completed in 2013. This was delayed again to 2016, the end of the 30-year lifespan of the sarcophagus. The structure is being built adjacent to the existing shelter and will be slid into place on rails. It is to be a metal arch 105 meters (344 ft) high and spanning 257 meters (843 ft), to cover both unit 4 and the hastily built 1986 structure. The Chernobyl Shelter Fund, set up in 1997, has received €810 million from international donors and projects to cover this project and previous work. It and the Nuclear Safety Account, also applied to Chernobyl decommissioning, are managed by the European Bank for Reconstruction and Development (EBRD).[citation needed]

By 2002, roughly 15,000 Ukrainian workers were still working within the Zone of Exclusion, maintaining the plant and performing other containment- and research-related tasks, often in dangerous conditions.[166]:2 A handful of Ukrainian scientists work inside the sarcophagus, but outsiders are rarely granted access. In 2006 an Australian 60 Minutes team led by reporter Richard Carleton and producer Stephen Rice were allowed to enter the sarcophagus for 15 minutes and film inside the control room.[170]

On 12 February 2013 a 600 m² (6,500 sq ft) section of the roof of the turbine-building, adjacent to the sarcophagus, collapsed. At first it was assumed that the roof collapsed because of the weight of snow on it. However the amount of snow was not exceptional, and the report of a Ukrainian fact-finding panel concluded that the part collapse of the turbine-building was the result of sloppy repair work and aging of the structure. The report mentioned the possibility that the repaired part of the turbine-building added a larger strain on the total structure than expected, and the braces in the roof were damaged by corrosion and sloppy welding. Experts such as Valentin Kupny, former deputy director of the nuclear plant, did warn that the complex was on the verge of a collapse, leaving the building in an extremely dangerous condition. A proposed reinforcement in 2005 was cancelled by a superior official. After the 12 February incident, radiation levels were up to 19 becquerels per cubic meter of air: 12 times normal. The report assumed radioactive materials from inside the structure spread to the surroundings after the roof collapsed. All 225 workers employed by the Chernobyl complex and the French company that is building the new shelter were evacuated shortly after the collapse. According to the managers of the complex, radiation levels around the plant were at normal levels (between 5 and 6 mS/h) and should not affect workers' health. According to Kupny the situation was underestimated by the Chernobyl nuclear complex managers, and information was kept secret.[171][172]

Radioactive materials and waste management

As of 2006, some fuel remained in the reactors at units 1 through 3, most of it in each unit's cooling pond, as well as some material in a small spent fuel interim storage facility pond (ISF-1).

In 1999 a contract was signed for construction of a radioactive waste management facility to store 25,000 used fuel assemblies from units 1–3 and other operational wastes, as well as material from decommissioning units 1–3 (which will be the first RBMK units decommissioned anywhere). The contract included a processing facility able to cut the RBMK fuel assemblies and to put the material in canisters, which were to be filled with inert gas and welded shut.

74

The canisters were to be transported to dry storage vaults, where the fuel containers would be enclosed for up to 100 years. This facility, treating 2500 fuel assemblies per year, would be the first of its kind for RBMK fuel. However, after a significant part of the storage structures had been built, technical deficiencies in the concept emerged, and the contract was terminated in 2007. The interim spent fuel storage facility (ISF-2) will now be completed by others by mid-2013.[citation needed]

Another contract has been let for a liquid radioactive waste treatment plant, to handle some 35,000 cubic meters of low- and intermediate-level liquid wastes at the site. This will need to be solidified and eventually buried along with solid wastes on site.[citation needed]

In January 2008, the Ukrainian government announced a 4-stage decommissioning plan that incorporates the above waste activities and progresses towards a cleared site .[94]

Lava-like fuel-containing materials (FCMs)

Main article: Corium (nuclear reactor)

According to official estimates, about 95% of the fuel in Reactor 4 at the time of the accident (about 180 metric tons) remains inside the shelter, with a total radioactivity of nearly 18 million curies (670 PBq). The radioactive material consists of core fragments, dust, and lava-like "fuel containing materials" (FCM, also called "corium") that flowed through the wrecked reactor building before hardening into a ceramic form.

Three different lavas are present in the basement of the reactor building: black, brown, and a porous ceramic. The lava materials are silicate glasses with inclusions of other materials within them. The porous lava is brown lava that dropped into water and thus cooled rapidly.

It is unclear how long the ceramic form will retard the release of radioactivity. From 1997 to 2002 a series of published papers suggested that the self-irradiation of the lava would convert all 1,200 metric tons into a sub micrometer and mobile powder within a few weeks.[173] But it has been reported that the degradation of the lava is likely to be a slow and gradual process rather than sudden and rapid.[174] The same paper states that the loss of uranium from the wrecked reactor is only 10 kg (22 lb) per year; this low rate of uranium leaching suggests that the lava is resisting its environment.[174] The paper also states that when the shelter is improved, the leaching rate of the lava will decrease.[174]

Some of the surfaces of the lava flows have started to show new uranium minerals such as Na
$_4$(UO
$_2$)(CO
$_3$)
$_3$ and uranyl carbonate. However, the level of radioactivity is such that during 100 years, the lava's self-irradiation (2×10^{16} α decays per gram and 2 to 5×10^5 Gy of β or γ) will fall short of the level required to greatly change the properties of glass (10^{18} α decays per gram and 10^8 to 10^9 Gy of β or γ). Also the lava's rate of dissolution in water is very low (10^{-7} g-cm^{-2} day^{-1}), suggesting that the lava is unlikely to dissolve in water.[174]

The Exclusion Zone

Chernobyl Exclusion Zone

Entrance to the zone of alienation around Chernobyl

An area originally extending 30 kilometres (19 mi) in all directions from the plant is officially called the "zone of alienation". It is largely uninhabited, except for about 300 residents who have refused to leave. The area has largely reverted to forest, and has been overrun by wildlife because of a lack of competition with humans for space and resources. Even today, radiation levels are so high that the workers responsible for rebuilding the sarcophagus are only allowed to work five hours a day for one month before taking 15 days of rest. Ukrainian officials estimate the area will not be safe for human life again for another 20,000 years.[56]

In 2011 Ukraine opened up the sealed zone around the Chernobyl reactor to tourists who wish to learn more about the tragedy that occurred in 1986.[175][176]

Recovery projects

The Chernobyl Shelter Fund

The Chernobyl Shelter Fund was established in 1997 at the Denver 23rd G8 summit to finance the Shelter Implementation Plan (SIP). The plan calls for transforming the site into an ecologically safe condition by means of stabilization of the sarcophagus followed by construction of a New Safe Confinement (NSC). While the original cost estimate for the SIP was US$768 million, the 2006 estimate was $1.2 billion. The SIP is being managed by a consortium of Bechtel, Battelle, and Electricité de France, and conceptual design for the NSC consists of a movable arch, constructed away from the shelter to avoid high radiation, to be slid over the sarcophagus. The NSC is expected to be completed in 2015,[177] and will be the largest movable structure ever built.

Dimensions:

- Span: 270 m (886 ft)
- Height: 100 m (330 ft)
- Length: 150 m (492 ft)

The United Nations Development Program

The United Nations Development Program has launched in 2003 a specific project called the Chernobyl Recovery and Development Program (CRDP) for the recovery of the affected areas.[178] The program was initiated in February 2002 based on the recommendations in the report on Human Consequences of the Chernobyl Nuclear Accident. The main goal of the CRDP's activities is supporting the Government of Ukraine in mitigating long-term social, economic, and ecological consequences of the Chernobyl catastrophe. CRDP works in the four most Chernobyl-affected areas in Ukraine: Kyivska, Zhytomyrska, Chernihivska and Rivnenska.

The International Project on the Health Effects of the Chernobyl Accident

The International Project on the Health Effects of the Chernobyl Accident (IPEHCA) was created and received US $20 million, mainly from Japan, in hopes of discovering the main cause of health problems due to ^{131}I radiation. These funds were divided between Ukraine, Belarus, and Russia, the three main affected countries, for further investigation of health effects. As there was significant corruption in former Soviet countries, most of the foreign aid was given to Russia, and no positive outcome from this money has been demonstrated.[citation needed]

Commemoration

Soviet badge awarded to liquidators

200,000 karbovanets coin issued by the National Bank of Ukraine to commemorate the 10th anniversary of the Chernobyl disaster

The Front Veranda (1986), a lithograph by Susan Dorothea White in the National Gallery of Australia,[179] exemplifies worldwide awareness of the event. *Heavy Water: A Film for Chernobyl* was released by Seventh Art in 2006 to commemorate the disaster through poetry and first-hand accounts.[180] The film secured the Cinequest Award as well as the Rhode Island "best score" award[181] along with a screening at Tate Modern.[182]

Chernobyl Way is an annual rally run on 26 April by the opposition in Belarus as a remembrance of the Chernobyl disaster.

Cultural impact

The Chernobyl accident attracted a great deal of interest. Because of the distrust that many people (both within and outside the USSR) had in the Soviet authorities, a great deal of debate about the situation at the site occurred in the first world during the early days of the event. Because of defective intelligence based on photographs taken from space, it was thought that unit number three had also suffered a dire accident.[citation needed]

Journalists mistrusted many professionals (such as the spokesman from the UK NRPB), and in turn encouraged the public to mistrust them.[156]

In Italy, the Chernobyl accident was reflected in the outcome of the 1987 referendum. As a result of that referendum, Italy began phasing out its nuclear power plants in 1988, a decision that was effectively reversed in 2008. A referendum in 2011 reiterated Italians' strong objections to nuclear power, thus abrogating the government's decision of 2008.

References

1. Black, Richard (12 April 2011). *"Fukushima: As Bad as Chernobyl?"*. BBC. Retrieved 20 August 2011.
2. Gorbachev, Mikhail (1996), interview in Johnson, Thomas, *The Battle of Chernobyl* on *YouTube*, [film], Discovery Channel, retrieved 30 October 2012.
3. "Frequently Asked Chernobyl Questions". International Atomic Energy Agency – Division of Public Information. May 2005. Retrieved 23 March 2011.
4. "Table 2.2 Number of people affected by the Chernobyl accident (to December 2000)" (PDF). *The Human Consequences of the Chernobyl Nuclear Accident*. UNDP and UNICEF. 22 January 2002. p. 32. Retrieved 17 September 2010.
5. "Table 5.3: Evacuated and resettled people" (PDF). *The Human Consequences of the Chernobyl Nuclear Accident*. UNDP and UNICEF. 22 January 2002. p. 66. Retrieved 17 September 2010.
6. ICRIN Project (2011). *International Chernobyl Portal chernobyl.info*. Retrieved 2011.
7. *Environmental consequences of the Chernobyl accident and their remediation: Twenty years of experience. Report of the Chernobyl Forum Expert Group 'Environment'*. Vienna: International Atomic Energy Agency. 2006. p. 180. ISBN 92-0-114705-8. Retrieved 13 March 2011.
8. Kagarlitsky, Boris (1989). "Perestroika: The Dialectic of Change". In Mary Kaldor, Gerald Holden, Richard A. Falk. *The New Detente: Rethinking East-West Relations*. United Nations University Press. ISBN 0-86091-962-5.
9. Associated Press, 24 April 2006, at msnbc.msn.com

10. "Assessing the Chernobyl Consequences". International Atomic Energy Agency.
11. "UNSCEAR 2008 Report to the General Assembly, Annex D". United Nations Scientific Committee on the Effects of Atomic Radiation. 2008.
12. "UNSCEAR 2008 Report to the General Assembly". United Nations Scientific Committee on the Effects of Atomic Radiation. 2008.
13. Hallenbeck, William H (1994). *Radiation Protection*. CRC Press. p. 15. ISBN 0-87371-996-4. "Reported thus far are 237 cases of acute radiation sickness and 31 deaths."
14. "Chernobyl: the true scale of the accident". *Chernobyl's Legacy: Health, Environmental and Socio-Economic Impacts*. Retrieved 15 April 2011.
15. "Estimates of the cancer burden in Europe from radioactive fallout from the Chernobyl accident". Onlinelibrary.wiley.com. doi:10.1002/ijc.22037. Retrieved 2013-09-12.
16. Chernobyl Cancer Death Toll Estimate More Than Six Times Higher Than the 4,000 Frequently Cited, According to a New UCS Analysis Note: *"The UCS analysis is based on radiological data provided by UNSCEAR, and is consistent with the findings of the Chernobyl Forum and other researchers."*
17. "Torch: The Other Report On Chernobyl— executive summary". European Greens and UK scientists Ian Fairlie PhD and David Sumner – Chernobylreport.org. April 2006. Retrieved 20 August 2011.
18. http://www.greenpeace.org/international/Global/international/planet-2/report/2006/4/chernobylhealthreport.pdf
19. Alexey V. Yablokov; Vassily B. Nesterenko; Alexey V. Nesterenko (2009). *Chernobyl: Consequences of the Catastrophe for People and*

the Environment (Annals of the New York Academy of Sciences) (paperback ed.). Wiley-Blackwell. ISBN 978-1-57331-757-3.

20. Correspondence (see reference 17) to George Monbiot from Douglas Braaten, Director and Executive Editor, Annals of the New York Academy of Sciences, dated 2nd April 2011: *"In no sense did Annals of the New York Academy of Sciences or the New York Academy of Sciences commission this work; nor by its publication do we intend to independently validate the claims made in the translation or in the original publications cited in the work. The translated volume has not been peer-reviewed by the New York Academy of Sciences, or by anyone else."*

21. New York Academy of Sciences (2010-04-28). "Statement on Annals of the New York Academy of Sciences volume entitled "Chernobyl: Consequences of the Catastrophe for People and the Environment"". Retrieved 2011-09-15.

22. M. I. Balonov (28 April 2010). "Review of Volume 1181". New York Academy of Sciences. Retrieved 15 September 2011. Full text PDF

23. Medvedev, Zhores A. (1990). *The Legacy of Chernobyl* (Paperback. First American edition published in 1990 ed.). W. W. Norton & Company. ISBN 978-0-393-30814-3.

24. *DOE Fundamentals Handbook – Nuclear physics and reactor theory* (PDF). 1 of 2, module 1. United States Department of Energy. 61. Retrieved 3 June 2010.[dead link]

25. "Standard Review Plan for the Review of Safety Analysis Reports for Nuclear Power Plants: LWR Edition (NUREG-0800)". *United States Nuclear Regulatory Commission*. May 2010. Retrieved 2 June 2010.

26. NV Karpan: 312–13.
27. "IAEA Report INSAG-7 Chernobyl Accident: Updating of INSAG-1 Safety Series, No.75-INSAG-7". Vienna: International Atomic Energy Agency. 1992.
28. A.S.Djatlov:30
29. "Chapter I The site and accident sequence - Chernobyl: Assessment of Radiological and Health Impact". Oecd-nea.org. 1986-04-26. Retrieved 2013-09-12.
30. "The official program of the test" (in Russian).
31. A.S.Djatlov:31
32. "What Happened at Chernobyl?". Nuclear Fissionary. Retrieved 12 January 2011.
33. The accumulation of Xenon-135 in the core is burned out by neutrons. Thus, higher power settings, associated with higher neutron flux, burn the xenon out more quickly. Conversely, low power settings result in the accumulation of xenon.
34. The information on accident at the Chernobyl NPP and its consequences, prepared for IAEA, Atomic Energy, v. 61, 1986, p. 308–320.
35. The RBMK is a boiling water reactor, so in-core boiling is normal at higher power levels. The RBMK design has a negative void coefficient above 700 MW.
36. "Physicians of Chernobyl Association" (in Russian). Association «Physicians of Chernobyl». Retrieved September 3, 2013.
37. E. O. Adamov; Yu. M. Cherkashov, et al. (2006). *Channel Nuclear Power Reactor RBMK* (in Russian) (Hardcover ed.). Moscow: GUP NIKIET. ISBN 5-98706-018-4.
38. Dyatlov, Anatoly. "4". *Chernobyl. How did it happen?* (in Russian).
39. "Chernobyl as it was – 2" (in Russian).

40. Davletbaev, RI (1995). *Last shift Chernobyl. Ten years later. Inevitability or chance?* (in Russian). Moscow: Energoatomizdat. ISBN 5-283-03618-9.
41. "Chernobyl: Assessment of Radiological and Health Impact (Chapter 1)". Nuclear Energy Agency. Retrieved 20 August 2011.
42. Checherov, K.P. (25–7 November 1998). *Development of ideas about reasons and processes of emergency on the 4-th unit of Chernobyl NPP 26.04.1986* (in Russian). Slavutich, Ukraine: International conference "Shelter-98".
43. Pakhomov, Sergey A.; Dubasov, Yuri V. (2009). "Estimation of Explosion Energy Yield at Chernobyl NPP Accident". *Pure and Applied Geophysics* **167** (4–5): 575. doi:10.1007/s00024-009-0029-9.
44. B. Medvedev (June 1989). "JPRS Report: Soviet Union Economic Affairs Chernobyl Notebook" (Republished by the Foreign Broadcast Information Service ed.). Novy Mir. Retrieved 27 March 2011.
45. "Cross-sectional view of the RBMK-1000 main building". Retrieved 11 September 2010.
46. Medvedev, Grigori (1989). *The Truth About Chernobyl* (Hardcover. First American edition published by Basic Books in 1991 ed.). VAAP. ISBN 2-226-04031-5.
47. National Geographic (2004). *Meltdown in Chernobyl* (Video).
48. Shcherbak, Y (1987). Medvedev, ed. *Chernobyl* **6**. Yunost. p. 44.
49. Adam Higginbotham (26 March 2006). "Adam Higginbotham: Chernobyl 20 years on | World news | The Observer". *The Guardian* (London). Retrieved 22 March 2010.
50. *Mil Mi-8 crash near Chernobyl* (Video). 2006.

51. *"Special Report: 1997: Chernobyl: Containing Chernobyl?"*. BBC News. 21 November 1997. Retrieved 20 August 2011.

52. Zeilig, Martin (August/September 1995). "Louis Slotin And 'The Invisible Killer'". *The Beaver* **75** (4): 20–27. Retrieved 28 April 2008.

53. National Geographic, VOL. 171, NO. 5, May 1987 (article "Chernobyl – One Year After")

54. "Веб публикация статей газеты". Swrailway.gov.ua. Retrieved 22 March 2010.

55. "Методическая копилка" (in russian). Surkino.edurm.ru. Retrieved 22 March 2010.

56. *Time: Disasters that Shook the World*. New York City: Time Home Entertainment. 2012. ISBN 1-60320-247-1.

57. **(Russian)** Video footage of Chernobyl disaster on 28 April on YouTube

58. **(English)** American TV-footage about Chernobyl

59. "Chernobyl haunts engineer who alerted world". *CNN Interactive World News* (Cable News Network, Inc.). 26 April 1996. Retrieved 28 April 2008.

60. Director: Maninderpal Sahota; Narrator: Ashton Smith; Producer: Greg Lanning; Edited by: Chris Joyce (17 August 2004). *"Seconds From Disaster"*. *Seconds From Disaster*. Season 1 (2004). Episode 7. 30/40–50 minutes in. National Geographic Channel.

61. "Interview of Valentyna Shevchenko to "Young Ukraine" (Ukrainian Pravda)". Istpravda.com.ua. 25 April 2011. Retrieved 20 August 2011.

62. **(Ukrainian)** Presidential Decree #501/2011 "For distinguishing with the state awards of Ukraine"

63. **(Ukrainian)** Presidential Decree #502/2011 "For distinguishing with the state awards of Ukraine the citizens of foreign countries"

64. Bogatov, S. A.; Borovoi, A. A.; Lagunenko, A. S.; Pazukhin, E. M.; Strizhov, V. F.; Khvoshchinskii, V. A. (2009). "Formation and spread of Chernobyl lavas". *Radiochemistry* **50** (6): 650. doi:10.1134/S1066362208050131.

65. Petrov, Yu. B.; Udalov, Yu. P.; Subrt, J.; Bakardjieva, S.; Sazavsky, P.; Kiselova, M.; Selucky, P.; Bezdicka, P.; Jorneau, C.; Piluso, P. (2009). "Behavior of melts in the UO2-SiO2 system in the liquid-liquid phase separation region". *Glass Physics and Chemistry* **35** (2): 199. doi:10.1134/S1087659609020126.

66. Journeau, C.; E. Boccaccio, C. Jégou, P. Piluso, G. Cognet (2001). "Flow and Solidification of Corium in the VULCANO facility". *5th World conference on experimental heat transfer, fluid mechanics and thermodynamics, Thessaloniki, Greece.*

67. Mevedev Z. (1990):58–59[*full citation needed*]

68. "Stephen McGinty: Lead coffins and a nation's thanks for the Chernobyl suicide squad". scotsman.com. 16 March 2011.

69. Chernobyl: The End of the Nuclear Dream, 1986, p.178, by Nigel Hawkes et al., ISBN 0-330-29743-0

70. Sattonnay, G.; Ardois, C.; Corbel, C.; Lucchini, J.F.; Barthe, M.-F.; Garrido, F.; Gosset, D. (2001). "Alpha-radiolysis effects on UO2 alteration in water". *Journal of Nuclear Materials* **288**: 11. doi:10.1016/S0022-3115(00)00714-5.

71. Casas, I.; Giménez, J.; Rovira, M. (2004). "Formation of Studtite during the Oxidative Dissolution of UO2by Hydrogen Peroxide: A SFM Study". *Environmental Science & Technology* **38** (24): 6656. doi:10.1021/es0492891.

72. Burakov, B. E.; Strykanova, E. E.; Anderson, E. B. (2012). "Secondary Uranium Minerals on the

Surface of Chernobyl "Lava"". *MRS Proceedings* **465**. doi:10.1557/PROC-465-1309.

73. Burns, P. C; K. A Hughes (2003). "Studtite, (UO2)(O2)(H2O)2(H2O)2: The first structure of a peroxide mineral". *American Mineralogist* **88** (7): 1165–1168.

74. Tom Burnett (28 March 2011). "When the Fukushima Meltdown Hits Groundwater". Hawai'i News Daily.

75. The Social Impact of the Chernobyl Disaster, 1988, p. 166, by David R. Marples ISBN 0-333-48198-4

76. Collecting History (1986-04-26). "Medal for Service at the Chernobyl Nuclear Disaster". Collectinghistory.net. Retrieved 2013-09-12.

77. "Chernobyl's silent graveyards". *BBC News*. 20 April 2006.

78. IAEA Report INSAG-1 (International Nuclear Safety Advisory Group). Summary Report on the Post-Accident Review on the Chernobyl Accident. Safety Series No. 75-INSAG-1.IAEA, Vienna, 1986.

79. **(Russian)***Expert report to the IAEA on the Chernobyl accident* **61**. Atomic Energy. 1986.

80. "INSAG-7 The Chernobyl Accident: Updating of INSAG-1" (PDF). Retrieved 2013-09-12.

81. "Chernobyl - Assessment of Radiological and Health Impacts" (PDF). Retrieved 2013-09-12.

82. Chernobyl Accident

83. "NEI Source Book: Fourth Edition (NEISB_3.3.A1)". Insc.anl.gov. Retrieved 31 July 2010.

84. "Facts: The accident was by far the most devastating in the history of nuclear power". *Ten years after Chernobyl : What do we really know?*. International Atomic Energy Agency (IAEA). 21 September 1997. Retrieved 20 August 2011.

85. Marples, David R. (May/June 1996). "The Decade of Despair". *The Bulletin of the Atomic Scientists* **52** (3): 20–31.
86. "Tchernobyl, 20 ans après" (in French). RFI. 24 April 2006. Retrieved 24 April 2006.
87. "L'accident et ses conséquences: Le panache radioactif" [The accident and its consequences: The plume] (in French). Institut de Radioprotection et de Sûreté Nucléaire (IRSN). Retrieved 16 December 2006.
88. Jensen, Mikael; Lindhé, John-Christer (Autumn 1986). "International Reports – Sweden: Monitoring the Fallout". *IAEA Bulletin* (International Atomic Energy Agency (IAEA))
89. Mould, Richard Francis (2000). *Chernobyl Record: The Definitive History of the Chernobyl Catastrophe*. CRC Press. p. 48. ISBN 0-7503-0670-X.
90. Ikäheimonen, T.K. (ed.). *Ympäristön Radioaktiivisuus Suomessa – 20 Vuotta Tshernobylista [Environmental Radioactivity in Finland - 20 Years from Chernobyl]*. Säteilyturvakeskus Stralsäkerhetscentralen (STUK, Radiation and Nuclear Safety Authority)
91. "3.1.5. Deposition of radionuclides on soil surfaces" (PDF). *Environmental Consequences of the Chernobyl Accident and their Remediation: Twenty Years of Experience, Report of the Chernobyl Forum Expert Group 'Environment'*. Vienna: International Atomic Energy Agency (IAEA). 2006. pp. 23–25. ISBN 92–0–114705–8 Check |isbn= value (help). Retrieved 2013-09-12.
92. Gould, Peter (1990). *Fire In the Rain: The Dramatic Consequences of Chernobyl*. Baltimore, MD: Johns Hopkins Press.

93. Gray, Richard (22 April 2007). "How we made the Chernobyl rain". *Telegraph* (London). Retrieved 27 November 2009.

94. "Chernobyl Accident 1986". World Nuclear Association. May 2008. Retrieved 18 June 2008.

95. Dederichs, Herbert; Pillath, Jürgen; Heuel-Fabianek, Burkhard; Hill, Peter; Lennartz, Reinhard (2009). "Langzeitbeobachtung der Dosisbelastung der Bevölkerung in radioaktiv kontaminierten Gebieten Weißrusslands – Korma-Studie" [Long-term monitoring of radiation exposure of the population in radioactively contaminated areas of Belarus - Korma Study]. *Schriften des Forschungszentrums Jülich: Reihe Energie & Umwelt / Energy & Environment* **31**. Forschungszentrum Jülich, Zentralbibliothek, Verlag. Retrieved 30 January 2011.

96. "Conséquences de la catastrophe de Tchernobyl en France". *French-speaking Wikipedia* (in French). Retrieved 18 March 2011.

97. "'Radioactive boars' on loose in Germany". *Agence France Presse*. August 2010. Retrieved 9 August 2010.[*dead link*]

98. Marples, David R. (1991). *Ukraine Under Perestroika: Ecology, Economics and the Workers' Revolt*. Basingstoke, Hampshire: MacMillan Press. pp. 50–51, 76.

99. J Wertelecki, W. (2010). "Malformations in a Chornobyl-Impacted Region". *Pediatrics* **125** (4): e836–43. doi:10.1542/peds.2009-2219. PMID 20308207.

100. Dancause, Kelsey Needham; Yevtushok, Lyubov; Lapchenko, Serhiy; Shumlyansky, Ihor; Shevchenko, Genadiy; Wertelecki, Wladimir; Garruto, Ralph M. (2010). "Chronic radiation exposure in the Rivne-Polissia region of Ukraine:

Implications for birth defects". *American Journal of Human Biology* **22** (5): 667–74. doi:10.1002/ajhb.21063. PMID 20737614.

101.   Møller, Anders Pape (April 1998). "Developmental Instability of Plants and Radiation from Chernobyl". *Oikos* (Nordic Ecological Society) **81** (3): 444–8. doi:10.2307/3546765. JSTOR 3546765.

102.   Saino, N.; Mousseau, F.; De Lope, T.A.; Saino, A.P. (2007). "Elevated frequency of abnormalities in barn swallows from Chernobyl". *Biology Letters* **3** (4): 414–7. doi:10.1098/rsbl.2007.0136. PMC 1994720. PMID 17439847.

103.   Weigelt, E.; Scherb, H. (2004). "Spaltgeburtenrate in Bayern vor und nach dem Reaktorunfall in Tschernobyl". *Mund-, Kiefer- und Gesichtschirurgie* **8** (2): 106. doi:10.1007/s10006-004-0524-1.

104.   Bennett, Burton; Repacholi, Michael; Carr, Zhanat, eds. (2006). *Health Effects of the Chernobyl Accident and Special Health Care Programmes: Report of the UN Chernobyl Forum, Expert Group "Health"* (PDF). Geneva: World Health Organization (WHO). ISBN 978-92-4-159417-2. Retrieved 20 August 2011[*page needed*]

105.   ᵍ Chapter II The release, dispersion and deposition of radionuclides - Chernobyl: Assessment of Radiological and Health Impact. Oecd-nea.org. Retrieved on 2013-02-13.

106.   Chernobyl source term, atmospheric dispersion, and dose estimation, *EnergyCitationsDatabase*, 1 November 1989

107.   OECD Papers Volume 3 Issue 1, *OECD*, 2003

108.	"The Society for Radiological Protection - SRP". Srp-uk.org. Retrieved 2013-09-12.

109.	"Applet for kids". Colorado.edu. 1999-09-20. Retrieved 2013-09-12.

110.	Ken Lyle. "Mathematical half life decay rate equations". Chem.purdue.edu. Retrieved 2013-09-12.

111.	"Unfall im japanischen Kernkraftwerk Fukushima". ZAMG. 24 March 2011. Retrieved 20 August 2011.

112.	Cesium-137: A Deadly Hazard. Large.stanford.edu (2012-03-20). Retrieved on 2013-02-13.

113.	Mould 2000, p. 29. "The number of deaths in the first three months were 31[.]"

114.	Marples, David R. (1988). *The Social Impact of the Chernobyl Disaster*. New York, NY: St Martin's Press.

115.	Chernobyl: Catastrophe and Consequences, Springer, Berlin ISBN 3-540-23866-2

116.	Kryshev, I.I. (1995). "Radioactive contamination of aquatic ecosystems following the Chernobyl accident". *Journal of Environmental Radioactivity* **27** (3): 207. doi:10.1016/0265-931X(94)00042-U.

117.	EURATOM Council Regulations No. 3958/87, No. 994/89, No. 2218/89, No. 770/90

118.	Fleishman, David G.; Nikiforov, Vladimir A.; Saulus, Agnes A.; Komov, Victor T. (1994). "137Cs in fish of some lakes and rivers of the Bryansk region and north-west Russia in 1990–1992". *Journal of Environmental Radioactivity* **24** (2): 145. doi:10.1016/0265-931X(94)90050-7.

119.	"Environmental consequences of the Chernobyl accident and their remediation" PDF IAEA, Vienna

120.   *Wildlife defies Chernobyl radiation*, by Stefen Mulvey, BBC News

121.   The International Chernobyl Project Technical Report, IAEA, Vienna, 1991

122.   "'Radiation-Eating' Fungi Finding Could Trigger Recalculation Of Earth's Energy Balance And Help Feed Astronauts".

123.   "25 Jahre Tschernobyl: Deutsche Wildschweine immer noch verstrahlt – Nachrichten Wissenschaft – WELT ONLINE". *Die Welt* (in **(German)**). 18 March 2011. Retrieved 20 August 2011.

124.   Rosslyn Beeby (27 April 2011). "World's nuclear power industry in decline". *Canberra Times*.

125.   "Record low number of radioactive sheep". *The Local* (The Local Europe AB). 23 September 2013. Retrieved 1 November 2013.

126.   "Fortsatt nedforing etter radioaktivitet i dyr som har vært på utmarksbeite – Statens landbruksforvaltning". SLF. 30 June 2010. Retrieved 20 August 2011.

127.   Macalister, Terry; Helen Carter (12 May 2009). "Britain's farmers still restricted by Chernobyl nuclear fallout". *The Guardian*. Retrieved 1 November 2013.

128.   Rawlinson, Kevin; Rachel Hovenden (7 July 2010). "Scottish sheep farms finally free of Chernobyl fallout". *The Independent*. Retrieved 1 November 2013.

129.   "Post-Chernobyl disaster sheep controls lifted on last UK farms". *BBC News* (BBC). 1 June 2012. Retrieved 1 November 2013.

130.   Food Standards Agency (29 November 2012). "Welsh sheep controls revoked". Retrieved 1 November 2013.

131.	"Chernobyl Forum summaries". International Atomic Energy Agency. Retrieved 31 July 2010.

132.	"Chernobyl's Legacy: Health, Environmental and Socio-Economic Impacts". *Chernobyl Forum assessment report.* Chernobyl Forum. Retrieved 21 April 2012.

133.	Chernobyl: the true scale of the accident, Joint News Release WHO/IAEA/UNDP, 5 SEPTEMBER 2005

134.	"UNSCEAR – Chernobyl health effects". Unscear.org. Retrieved 23 March 2011.

135.	Rosenthal, Elisabeth. (6 September 2005) Experts find reduced effects of Chernobyl. Nytimes.com. Retrieved 14 February 2008.

136.	"Thyroid Cancer". Genzyme.ca. Retrieved 31 July 2010.

137.	"CHERNOBYL at 25th anniversary Frequently Asked Questions April 2011". World Health Organisation. 23 April 2011. Retrieved 14 April 2012.

138.	"Chernobyl's Legacy: Health, Environmental and Socia-Economic Impacts and Recommendations to the Governments of Belarus, Russian Federation and Ukraine" (PDF). International Atomic Energy Agency – The Chernobyl Forum: 2003–2005. Retrieved 31 July 2010.

139.	"Excerpt from UNSCEAR 2001 REPORT ANNEX – Hereditary effects of radiation" (PDF). Retrieved 20 August 2011.

140.	Bogdanova TI, Zurnadzhy LY, Greenebaum E, McConnell RJ, Robbins J, Epstein OV, Olijnyk VA, Hatch M, Zablotska LB, Tronko MD. (2006). "A cohort study of thyroid cancer and other thyroid diseases after the Chornobyl accident: pathology analysis of thyroid cancer cases in Ukraine detected during the first screening (1998–2000)". *Cancer* **11** (107): 2599–66. doi:10.1002/cncr.22321. PMC 2983485. PMID 17083123.

141.   Dinets A, Hulchiy M, Sofiadis A, Ghaderi M, Höög A, Larsson C, Zedenius J. (2012). "Clinical, Genetic and Immunohistochemical Characterization of 70 Ukrainian Adult Cases with Post-Chornobyl Papillary Thyroid Carcinoma". *Eur J Endocrinol* **166** (6): 1049–60. doi:10.1530/EJE-12-0144. PMC 3361791. PMID 22457234.

142.   "20 years after Chernobyl – The ongoing health effects". *IPPNW*. April 2006. Retrieved 24 April 2006.

143.   Mettler, Fred. "IAEA Bulletin Volume 47, No. 2 – Chernobyl's Legacy". Iaea.org. Retrieved 20 August 2011.

144.   "What's the situation at Chernobyl?". Iaea.org. Retrieved 20 August 2011.

145.   Mettler, Fred. "Chernobyl's living legacy". Iaea.org. Retrieved 20 August 2011.

146.   "UNSCEAR assessment of the Chernobyl accident". United Nations Scientific Committee of the Effects of Atomic Radiation. Retrieved 31 July 2010.

147.   "Historical milestones". United Nations Scientific Committee of the Effects of Atomic Radiation. Retrieved 14 April 2012.

148.   World Health Organisation "World Health Organization report explains the health impacts of the world's worst-ever civil nuclear accident", *WHO*, 26 April 2006. Retrieved 4 April 2011.

149.   Berrington De González, Amy; Mahesh, M; Kim, KP; Bhargavan, M; Lewis, R; Mettler, F; Land, C (2009). "Projected Cancer Risks from Computed Tomographic Scans Performed in the

United States in 2007". *Archives of Internal Medicine* **169** (22): 2071–7. doi:10.1001/archinternmed.2009.440. PMID 20008689.

150.   Normile, D. (2011). "Fukushima Revives the Low-Dose Debate". *Science* **332** (6032): 908–10. doi:10.1126/science.332.6032.908. PMID 21596968.

151.   "How Many Cancers Did Chernobyl Really Cause?". UCSUSA.org. 17 April 2011.

152.   "The Chernobyl Catastrophe – Consequences on Human Health". Greenpeace. 18 April 2006. Retrieved 15 December 2008.

153.   Hawley, Charles. "Greenpeace vs. the United Nations". *The Chernobyl Body Count Controversy*. SPIEGEL. Retrieved 15 March 2011.

154.   "Details". *Annals of the New York Academy of Sciences*. Annals of the New York Academy of Sciences. Retrieved 15 March 2011.

155.   pp. 85-86, pp. 92-93 in "Radiation: What It Is, What You Need To Know" by Robert Peter Gale, M.D., Ph.D. and Eric Lax. Publisher: Alfred A. Knopf, New York, 2013. ("The correct number of Chernobyl-related cancers will never be known, in part because of the considerable uncertainties in estimating cancers and cancer deaths. Especially problematic is the controversy about whether very low doses of radiation, especially if given over a prolonged interval, increase cancer risk. There are other difficulties as well. For one, we do not know precisely what radiation dose most people received. People who were indoors when the radioactive plume passed received much less radiation than those who were outdoors. However, because most people did not know when the radioactive plume passed, they cannot accurately reconstruct their

whereabouts at that time. Also, many people were evacuated from contaminated land at different times and thus received very different doses from ground and food contamination. Next we have the geopolitical reality that many of the exposed people no longer live in the Chernobyl area. Living elsewhere, even in other countries, they are lost to follow-up. The Chernobyl accident was relatively quickly followed by the dissolution of the Soviet Union, whereupon many people's lifestyles but perhaps not their lives changed, mostly for the worse. For example, cigarette smoking and alcohol consumption increased, resulting in a profound drop in life expectancy. Both activities are correlated with increased cancer risk independent of radiation exposure. Sorting out any changes in cancer incidence or prevalence will be difficult at best. [...] Fourth, high-quality cancer registries were absent before and even after the accident, making it impossible to know with certainty the background rate of most cancers before the accident.")

156.   Kasperson, Roger E.; Stallen, Pieter Jan M. (1991). *Communicating Risks to the Public: International Perspectives*. Berlin: Springer Science and Media. pp. 160–162. ISBN 0-7923-0601-5.
157.   Knudsen, LB (1991). "Legally induced abortions in Denmark after Chernobyl". *Biomedicine & Pharmacotherapy* **45** (6): 229–31. doi:10.1016/0753-3322(91)90022-L. PMID 1912378.
158.   Trichopoulos, D; Zavitsanos, X; Koutis, C; Drogari, P; Proukakis, C; Petridou, E (1987). "The victims of chernobyl in Greece: Induced abortions after the accident". *British Medical Journal* **295** (6606): 1100. doi:10.1136/bmj.295.6606.1100. PMC 1248180. PMID 3120899.

159.   Parazzini, F; Repetto, F; Formigaro, M; Fasoli, M; La Vecchia, C (1988). "Induced abortions after the Chernobyl accident". *British Medical Journal* **296** (6615): 136. doi:10.1136/bmj.296.6615.136-a. PMC 2544742. PMID 3122957.

160.   Perucchi, M; Domenighetti, G (1990). "The Chernobyl accident and induced abortions: Only one-way information". *Scandinavian Journal of Work, Environment & Health* **16** (6): 443–4. doi:10.5271/sjweh.1761. PMID 2284594.

161.   ASU school of life scientist:Kenneth Mossman[*dead link*]

162.   Mossman, Kenneth L. (1998). "The linear no-threshold debate: Where do we go from here?". *Medical Physics* **25** (3): 279–84; discussion 300. doi:10.1118/1.598208. PMID 9547494.

163.   Shkolnikov, V.; McKee, M; Vallin, J; Aksel, E; Leon, D; Chenet, L; Meslé, F (1999). "Cancer mortality in Russia and Ukraine: Validity, competing risks and cohort effects". *International Journal of Epidemiology* **28** (1): 19–29. doi:10.1093/ije/28.1.19. PMID 10195659.

164.   Shlyakhter, Alexander; Wilson, Richard (1992). "Chernobyl andGlasnost: The Effects of Secrecy on Health and Safety". *Environment: Science and Policy for Sustainable Development* **34** (5): 25. doi:10.1080/00139157.1992.9931445.

165.   Petryna, Adriana (1995). "Sarcophagus: Chernobyl in Historical Light". *Cultural Anthropology* **10** (2): 196. doi:10.1525/can.1995.10.2.02a00030.

166.   Petryna, Adriana (2002). *Life Exposed: Biological Citizens after Chernobyl*. Princeton, NJ: Princeton University Press.

167. "Information Notice No. 93-71". Nrc.gov. Retrieved 20 August 2011.

168. IAEA's Power Reactor Information System polled in May 2008 reports shut down for units 1, 2, 3 and 4 respectively at 30 November 1996, 11 October 1991, 15 December 2000 and 26 April 1986.

169. Чернобыль, Припять, Чернобыльская АЭС и зона отчуждения. ""Shelter" object description". Chornobyl.in.ua. Retrieved 8 May 2012.

170. "Inside Chernobyl". 60 Minutes Australia, Nine Network Australia. 16 April 2006.

171. "Collapse of Chernobyl nuke plant building attributed to sloppy repair work, aging". *The Mainichi Newspapers*. 25 April 25, 2013. Retrieved 26 April 2013.

172. Ukraine: Chernobyl nuclear roof collapse 'no danger', BBC News, 13 February 2013

173. Baryakhtar, V.; Gonchar, V.; Zhidkov, A.; Zhidkov, V. (2002). "Radiation damages and self-sputtering of high-radioactive dielectrics: spontaneous emission of submicronic dust particles". *Condensed Matter Physics* **5** (3{31}): 449–471.

174. Borovoi, A. A. (2006). "Nuclear fuel in the shelter". *Atomic Energy* **100** (4): 249. doi:10.1007/s10512-006-0079-3.

175. "News". Yahoo News. Associated Press. 13 December 2010. Retrieved 2 March 2012.

176. "Tours of Chernobyl sealed zone officially begin". TravelSnitch. TravelSnitch. 18 March 2011.

177. "NOVARKA and Chernobyl Project Management Unit confirm cost and time schedule for Chernobyl New Safe Confinement". 8 April 2011. Retrieved 28 March 2012.

178.   "CRDP: Chernobyl Recovery and Development Programme (United Nations Development Programme)". Undp.org.ua. Retrieved 31 July 2010.

179.   ""The Front Veranda" (1986)". Susandwhite.com.au. Retrieved 2013-09-12.

180.   "Processing the Dark: *Heavy Water – A Film for Chernobyl* | Movie Mail UK". Moviemail-online.co.uk. Retrieved 31 July 2010.

181.   "online data source". Retrieved 6 August 2013.

182.   "Heavy Water: a film for Chernobyl". Atomictv.com. 26 April 1986. Retrieved 6 August 2013.

Graffiti adorns a wall April 4 in the ghost city of Pripyat near the fourth nuclear reactor (background) at the former Chernobyl Nuclear power plant, site of the world's worst nuclear disaster. (Sergei Supinsky/AFP/Getty Images)

The Chernobyl nuclear power plant sits crippled two to three days after the explosion in Chernobyl, Ukraine in April, 1986. In front of the chimney is the destroyed 4th reactor. (AP)

102

A helicopter sprays a decontaminate over the region surrounding the Chernobyl nuclear power station on June 13, 1986. (Reuters/Itar-Tass)

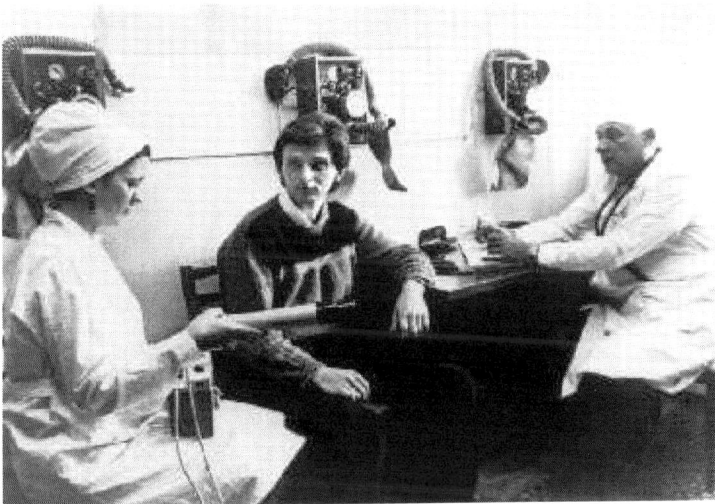

An engineer working at the Chernobyl plant is checked by doctors of the sanatorium of Lesnaya Polyana on May 15, 1986, a few days after the No. 4 reactor's blast. (Stf/AFP/Getty Images)

People hold a rally to protest against a Ukrainian initiative to cut social benefits for "liquidators", emergency workers who fought the blaze at the Chernobyl nuclear reactor, near the government's headquarters in Kiev on March 16. (Gleb Garanich/Reuters)

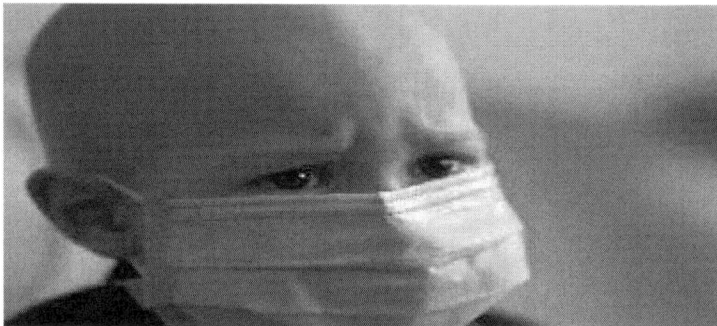

A child wears a mask in a hospital for leukemia patients in Donetsk, Ukraine on March 23. The blasts at the Soviet-era plant created a cloud of radioactive dust that drifted over a large swathe of Europe and still haunts millions of people in Ukraine and its neighbors. (Alexander Khudoteply/AFP/Getty Images)

A Ferris wheel sits abandoned in the deserted town of Pripyat, less than two miles from the Chernobyl nuclear power plant. (Sergey Ponomarev/AP)

A gas mask and children's toys gather dust in a kindergarten in the ghost city of Pripyat on April 4. (Sergei Supinsky/AFP/Getty Images)

Beds sit in disarray in a kindergarten in the ghost city of Pripyat on April 4. (Sergei Supinsky/AFP/Getty Images)

A man visits his ruined house in the 19-mile exclusion zone around the Chernobyl nuclear reactor in the abandoned village of Lomysh, Belarus on March 18. (Vasily Fedosenko/Reuters)

Seventy-two year old Natalia Makeenko (left) hugs eighty-two year old Galina Shcyuka in the abandoned village of Savichi on April 21, close to the 19-mile exclusion zone around the Chernobyl nuclear reactor. (Viktor Drachev/AFP/Getty Images)

Villagers dine in memory of Maria Borisenko, 76, at a cemetery in the 19-mile exclusion zone around the Chernobyl nuclear reactor in the abandoned village of Lomysh on March 18.

Lida Masanovitz, 74, a former nurse, was born and raised in the now-abandoned ghost town of Redkovka, Ukraine. She is now a pensioner earning 1,000 grivnia ($125) and gets no additional government support, despite living in a radition zone. (Diana Markosian/Redux Images)

Lida Masanovitz plants onions and radishes in a field in the ghost town village of Redkokva, Ukraine. After the Chernobyl accident in 1986, villagers were asked not to eat home grown food in risk of radiation. (Diana Markosian/Redux Images)

Lida Masanovitz stands beside her husband, MIkhail Masanovitz, 73, as she speaks to her daughter on the phone. After the Chernobyl accident on April 26, 1986, Masanovitz's daughter was hospitalized and treated for thyroid issues. An estimated 7 million people in the former Soviet republics of Belarus, Russia and Ukraine suffered from radiation-linked ailments, including thyroid and circulation problems after the accident. (Diana Markosian/Redux Images)

Lida Masanovitz sleeps beside her husband MIkhail Masanovitz in their home. The two met in the now ghost village of Redkovka, Ukraine 50 years ago. (Diana Markosian/Redux Images)

A Belarussian villager pushes a trolley in the village of Tulgovichi, near the 19-mile exclusion zone around the Chernobyl nuclear reactor on February 22. Today, the Belarus border region from which the locals were evacuated in 1986 is a weird, overgrown wilderness - teeming with wildlife but virtually devoid of people, its shops and homes fast disappearing under a tangle of foliage. The village of Tulgovichi, which once had about 1,000 inhabitants, is still home to a handful of pensioners who have stubbornly resisted moves to get them to leave. (Vasily Fedosenko/Reuters)

A hunter chases a fox just outside the 19-mile exclusion zone around the Chernobyl nuclear reactor near the village of Novosiolki, Belarus on January 11, 2009. Despite radiation levels, wildlife in and around the exclusion zone has been teeming since people left the area after the 1986 nuclear disaster. Wolves, foxes and raccoon dogs can be hunted all year around. (Vasily Fedosenko/Reuters) #

A worker feeds bison at the state radiation ecology reserve in the 19-mile exclusion zone around the Chernobyl nuclear reactor near the village of Babchin, Belarus on February 21. (Vasily Fedosenko/Reuters)

A deer stands in the state radiation ecology reserve in the 19-mile exclusion zone around the Chernobyl nuclear reactor near the village of Babchin, Belarus on March 18. Still inhospitable to humans, the Chernobyl exclusion zone - a contaminated 19-mile radius around the site of the nuclear reactor explosion - is now a nature reserve and teems with different wild animals. (Vasily Fedosenko/Reuters)

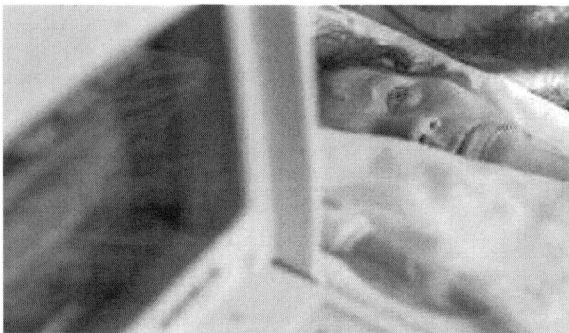

A woman is screened for thyroid cancer by doctors from the Red Cross in the village of Ukrainka, Ukraine on April 19. (Gleb Garanich/Reuters)

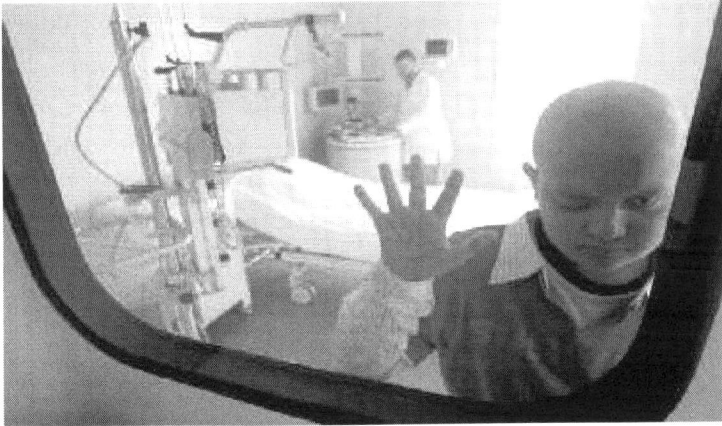

A cancer patient leans against the window of a special treatment chamber in a hospital in Donetsk, Ukraine on April 25, 2006. (Alexander Khudotioply/Reuters)

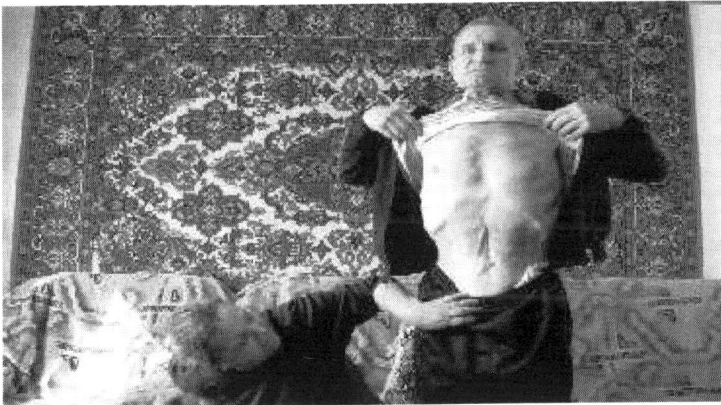

Viktor and Lydia Gaidak in their apartment in the Desnyanskiy district at the outskirts of Kyiv, Ukraine on April 27, 2007. Viktor Gaidak worked for 24 years as an engineer at the Chernobyl plant, including nine years after the 1986 accident. In 2004 he had surgery for colon cancer. (Michael Forster Rothbart)

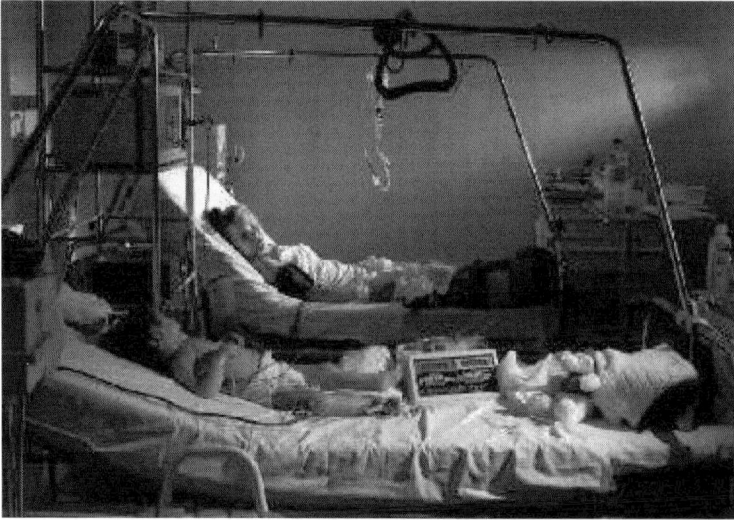

Olya Podoprigora, 13, and 18-month-old Parvana Sulemanova, recover in the ICU one day after open-heart surgeries in Kharkiv, Ukraine. Both girls had congenital heart defects, and every year, 6,000 children in Ukraine are born with genetic heart disease. Radiation is suspected as the cause, but is not proven. (Michael Forster Rothbart)

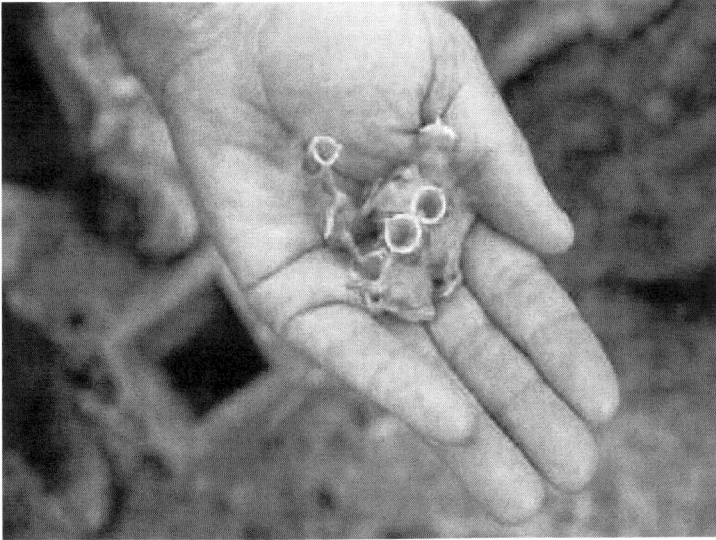

Ornithologist Igor Chizhebskiy holds a nestfull of newly hatched chicks on a wooded hilltop above the Chernobyl cooling pond. His research compares birth and survival rates of birds born in highly radioactive sites to those in less contaminated areas within the Zone. Surveys of birds, insects, and spiders by Igor and his colleagues indicate that many species are either absent or exist in very low numbers in the Chernobyl region. The diminished bird populations could be caused by radiation directly or may be due to a decrease in food sources such as insects. (Michael Forster Rothbart)

Late on a long winter's night, Nina Dubrovskaya and her friend
Lena Priyenko walk home to their village Sukachi, Ukraine, from
the nearby town of Ivankiv, 2 miles away. The two women, both
divorcees, went out to the bars in Ivankiv in search of company,
but found all 4 bars they visited nearly empty. "When the
money gets short, people just get drunk at home," says
Dubrovskaya. Sukachi is a village of 1,200. Half the people of
Sukachi are Chernobyl evacuees, relocated here from the
abandoned village of Ladizhichi. (Michael Forster Rothbart)

In Slavutych, Ukraine, a memorial hall in the city museum is dedicated to the Chernobyl accident, with photographs of the men and women who died immediately following the explosion. Former Chernobyl plant worker Sergii Kasyanchuk manages the Chernobyl Information Center museum now that his health no longer allows him to enter the Chernobyl Exclusion Zone. More than half the families in Slavutych have a member who still works at the plant, and everyone knows colleagues who became ill or died due to the Chernobyl accident. (Michael Forster Rothbart)

Teenage dancers wait backstage for their turn to perform during a Slavutych, Ukraine city concert. Slavutych is the new city built after the accident to house evacuated Chernobyl personnel. The Chernobyl plant once funded many programs in the city. Now the city struggles with decreased resources due to layoffs at the Chernobyl plant. (Michael Forster Rothbart)

A geiger counter shows a reading of the radiation levels in the air by the 4th power block of Chernobyl's nuclear power plant, covered with a "sarcophagus" as it lies derelict on March 31. (Sergei Supinsky/AFP/Getty Images)

Vehicles contaminated by radioactivity lay dormant on November 10, 2000 near the Chernobyl nuclear power plant. Some 1,350 Soviet military helicopters, buses, bulldozers, tankers, transporters, fire engines and ambulances were used while fighting the nuclear accident. All were irradiated during the clean-up operation. (Efrem Lukatsky/AP)

Employees of the Polessky State Radiation Ecological Reserve wear facemasks on April 20 as they plant trees on contaminated land near the abandoned village of Bogushi, Belarus, inside the 19-mile exclusion zone around the Chernobyl nuclear reactor, to form a natural windbreak to stop radioactive particles from blowing away. One-fifth of the country's agricultural land was contaminated following the blast at the nuclear reactor and around 70% of the fallout fell in Belarus. (Viktor Drachev/AFP/Getty Images)

Workers from the State Radiation Ecological Reserve test radiation levels on pigs at a farm in Vorotets, Belarus on April 21, close to the 19-mile exclusion zone around the Chernobyl nuclear reactor. (Viktor Drachev/AFP/Getty Images)

Schoolchildren wear gas masks during nuclear safety training lessons in Rudo, Ukraine near an isolated zone around the Chernobyl nuclear power plant April 3, 2006. (AP Photo/Sergey Ponomarev)

10811489R00068

Printed in Great Britain
by Amazon.co.uk, Ltd.,
Marston Gate.